KISS OFF CORPORATE AMERICA

KISS OFF CORPORATE AMERICA

A YOUNG PROFESSIONAL'S GUIDE TO INDEPENDENCE

Lisa Kivirist

Andrews McMeel
Publishing

Kansas City

www.andrewsmcmeel.com

Library of Congress Cataloging-in-Publication Data

Kivirist, Lisa
    Kiss off corporate America : a young professional's guide to independence / Lisa Kivirist.
        p.   cm.
    ISBN 0–8362–3590–8 (pbk.)
    1. Self-employed.   2. New business enterprises.   3. Entrepreneurship.
I. Title.
HD8036.K58   1998
658'.041—dc21   97–40973
                                                                CIP

98 99 00 01 02/BAH 10 9 8 7 6 5 4 3 2 1

ATTENTION: SCHOOLS AND BUSINESSES

Andrews McMeel books are available at quantity discounts with bulk purchase for educational, business, or sales promotional use. For information, please write to: Special Sales Department, Andrews McMeel Publishing, 4520 Main Street, Kansas City, Missouri 64111.

To Mom and Dad, for roots of love, and John, for wings.

ACKNOWLEDGMENTS

A book is not the sole effort of the author on the cover. I've been extremely fortunate to have been surrounded by a team of inspiring, supportive, butt-kicking people from the day the vision for this book cropped up in my mind. Thanks to Patty Rice, Jennifer Fox, and all at Andrews McMeel Publishing for believing in me and this book. Patty, thank you for always making me feel a contributing part of the process, and for empowering me with confidence in my writing ability. To my agent, Jeff Herman, for giving a wild card, first-time author your professional feedback, support, and vision. To Theresa DiGeronimo, for your professional support, advice, and polish. To my parents, for hanging in there with me through my own "kiss off" process. Thanks to all the people who shared their "kiss off" stories and visions; your candor will inspire others to follow their dreams. Through writing this book I once again realized the amazing people I have in my life, friends who have unwavering belief in my potential, even when all I want to do is pull the covers over my head. Thanks to Angela Carrales, Kara Belew, Caron Christy, David DeLong, Stephie Fine, Steven Glass, Adria Goodson, Laura Hankin, Beverly Haas, Susan Ivanko, Rob and Lisa Jillson, Sarah Kennedy, Debi Lewis, Bobby Lilly, Devoney Looser, Terri Reul, Magda and Endel Sang, Claire Simpson, Annie Stack, Jenni Taylor-Koval, Cheryl Toth, Leslie VanGelder, Suzi Wahl, Mara Walner, and Tom Walsh. Thanks for your feedback, ideas, listening to me vent at all hours, and hanging in there with me through my journey to "authordom." I'm indebted to Equal Exchange hazelnut java, Ben & Jerry's Chubby Hubby ice cream, the rain forests of Belize, and the beauty of Green County for inspiration. And most of all, to the one who jolts my life with passion, creativity, laughter, and the support to go after my dreams, my husband and partner, John.

CONTENTS

INTRODUCTION

*K*iss Off Corporate America: A Young Professional's Guide to Independence is a book about us, for us, and by us. Frankly, it's the book I needed to find during my bookstore browse sessions three years ago. The goal of this book is to be a catalyst, to encourage our "post-boomer" generation (too young to be boomers and not exactly Gen Xers), people early on in careers, to question what makes us unique and what will make us healthy and happy long-term. This book aims to encourage change and individuality, and to help you create a life/work style that is distinctly and uniquely your own.

In the next eight chapters, we'll go through step-by-step the various issues you'll need to consider while transitioning from the corporate to the self-employed sector. Some areas are pragmatic how-tos and resources, and others are more

> "You miss 100 percent of the shots you never take."
>
> —Wayne Gretzky

big-picture, philosophical questions to ask yourself. Keep reading for information on:

- how to prepare for self-employment while still at your corporate job
- various ways to pay the rent while pursuing your dream
- the pragmatics of setting up a business and home office
- financial planning for your future
- dealing with pressure and negative feedback from family and friends
- learning how to take care of and manage yourself through this process

Kiss Off Corporate America is designed to be a catalyst, a tool. Consider it an encyclopedia of suggestions. Thought-starters. Spark plugs. Jolts of self-employment espresso to get you going.

Congratulations! You've taken the first step. Set the gears in motion. Keep reading and dreaming—the best is yet to come. . . .

KISS OFF
CORPORATE
AMERICA

What's Brewing?

"If I'm Still Here When They Pass Out Those Gold Watches, Please Shoot Me"

When I did it, I got some different reactions. My boss gave me an eloquent, corporate "Huh?" My mother cried. I got a lot of blank stares. And, in the midst of it all, the chorus of "I could never do what you're doing, but I think it's great."

So what did I do? Bungee-jump without the cord? Sky-dive without the parachute? Swan-dive off the Empire State Building?

No, not exactly. At the ripe age of twenty-six, I left a cushy, lucrative, corporate benefit–lined advertising job for the chaotic, adventurous world of self-employment. I kissed off corporate America. Four years later, I don't regret my decision and wouldn't go back to a cubicle for all the gold watches in the IBM vault.

In the next eight chapters, you're going to hear my tale, as well as stories shared by many young professionals who have chosen to leave the corporate life for more meaningful, independent, entrepreneurial lives. The sources of these stories vary from people who, maybe like yourself, are just starting to think about all this, to people who are self-employed and financially supporting themselves. There are also people who have known for a while in the back of their mind that the corporate scene isn't for them, but they've been avoiding the "what to do with my life" analysis.

You'll hear from people who are newbies on the self-employment journey. What does it feel like to make your first moves into entrepreneurdom? What are some of the lessons they've learned along the way? And you'll also meet some seasoned folks who have created their personal lifestyles off the corporate track. How did they transform their life from cubicle confinement to one of self-employed freedom, independence, and creativity?

WHY DID I BUST OFF THE CORPORATE TRACK?

My decision to leave corporate America crept up on me slowly. It wasn't some lightning bolt of revelation that vividly popped into my brain one morning. Looking back, there were lots of subtle signs along the way:

- I started to see myself in the eyes of those older than I at the ad agency where I worked. I saw too many people at the office who had settled, who now had the 2.5 kids and stifling suburban mortgage, who had accepted the golden handcuffs the corporation had placed on them. I saw my future in them. Their dreams, their true selves, had been lost somewhere between the car loan and cellular phone. I didn't like what I was seeing in my crystal ball.

- I felt restless, though I didn't know exactly why. As I sat in my cubicle, my mind constantly wandered somewhere, anywhere, else. I developed an exceptionally creative repertoire of reasons to go to the supply room. Hey, at least I was going somewhere.

- I felt a lot of my important relationships slipping away. Sure, I had friends, good friends, but we were all in the same boat, spending our weekends drinking beer and bitching about work. Or escaping to the movies. Or running away to a weekend of blissful camping and camaraderie in Wisconsin, only to be slapped with reality (and the subtle guilt of not having worked the weekend) on Monday.

- I too often felt like a round peg trying to fit into a square hole. I could fit in splendidly. I could wear the right two-piece suit, inflect my voice at exactly the right presentation point, laugh at the right joke or at least fake it well. But I found myself letting more of the real me show outside of the work domain. Things that I did naturally for friends and people I cared about were not things that were encouraged or understood by corporate colleagues.

The problem with that is the same as walking around in shoes that don't fit: You can wear them, they will pinch every step of the way, and eventually your feet will become numb to the pain and you'll just blindly keep going. You've given up having something that fits you just right and settled with the familiarity of the status quo. You will have forgotten what it feels like to be in a situation that truly does fit the "real you."

SEARCHING FOR ANSWERS

Something in my life had to change. What frustrated me most, however, was that I didn't know what. I didn't know where to start. I didn't know if I needed a new haircut or a life overhaul. Realize that I am the type of person who always has a specific plan, step by anal step. I majored in X in college and did Y internship so I could get the job at Z company. I learned A by working for B years, C hours a day, and now what?

Does my story sound familiar? Are you too struggling with the "now what?" part? How do we know when "now" is? As a senior in college, I was so focused on getting that ideal first job (which I feel I did), that I never really thought about "now what?"

Now let me honestly admit that I had a good three years at this first job, and I don't at all regret what I did or feel that I made a wrong decision. There were a lot of exciting new things happening at that time. New job. New power suits. New apartment. New friends. New love. The fun social life in the city was fresh and exciting for some time.

However, corporate life year three was when the restless feelings hit. That's when I started dreading Mondays. This disturbed me because I had always considered myself a "take charge" person. If something is wrong, fix it. If there is something I want or don't want in my life, I do something about it. This situation frustrated me because I couldn't pinpoint what was wrong. I had seemingly achieved all I had set out to do and now had all the visuals of mid-twenties successes: the promotions, the salary, and the trendy mountain bike. What could be wrong?

I knew it wasn't simply advertising or the industry I was in; there are still many elements of the business that fascinate me. It wasn't simply the business world; I'm still a marketing junkie. So I spent many Saturday afternoons aimlessly searching the career guidance section at every bookstore in town. Sometimes I'd wander to the self-help section and poke around. Or the business section. But even with this buffet of resources, nothing was popping out as the right answer. My career taste buds were stagnant. Almost any alternative outside my cubicle looked so very appealing. I was overwhelmed with possibilities and couldn't move toward any of them. Was this a premature midlife crisis? My afternoon bookstore wanderings would often end at the local coffeehouse, bumping into friends who were as frustrated as I was, wallowing in corporate angst over high-quality caffeine.

I was searching for an answer, initially, a simple answer. I was looking for one of those color-coded quizzes that lead to the exact, right next step. I knew it wasn't simply a matter of revising my résumé, sending it out to different companies, and resurrecting padded interview answers. I wanted something else, something different. I didn't want the standard corporate track that society had placed such a high value on. I didn't want to be like everyone else, but at the same time, I was having a hard time discovering who this real, unique "me" was.

WHERE I AM NOW

And so I kissed off corporate America and lived successfully ever after. End of story, cue triumphant closing theme music. Stop! Cut the fantasy. My post–advertising agency life hardly falls into an easily digestible thirty-minute sitcom plot; it's more like a roller-coaster of chaos. But remember this: If I did it, you can.

It's been four years now since I left the cubicle and have been successfully self-employed. When people now ask me the "what do you do?" question, they had better pull up a comfortable chair and plan on sitting around awhile. My life no longer fits into a quick, one-sentence, cookie-cutter definition; I wear multiple hats and have a portfolio of projects on my plate. During those four years I started several businesses, bought a farm, traveled through three continents, got married, and never owed a dime of interest to Mr. Visa.

I started my own company, KivCo Communications, through which I work on a range of event marketing and advertising projects ranging from setting up Scotch whisky tastings to Earth Day environmental educational programs to bluebird conservation efforts. I teach introductory Macintosh and Internet classes at my local community college. My husband, John, and I are globe-trotters for extended periods of time, laptops in tow, doing a variety of travel-related writing and photography projects. We renovated a rural farmstead in Browntown, Wisconsin, and opened up a bed-and-breakfast called Inn Serendipity. On the farm, we grow most of our own fruits and vegetables, and we're exper-

"What is it that you want from me? You want me to get a job on the line for the next twenty years until I'm granted leave with my gold-plated watch and my balls full of tumors because I surrendered the one thing that means shit to me? Well, honey, you can just exhale because it ain't going to be in this lifetime."

—Troy, *Reality Bites*, Universal Pictures, 1994

imenting this year with growing organic sunflowers for cut-flower sales. I've been able to volunteer with organizations and causes important to me, primarily leadership training programs for high school students.

And over the past four years I've completed a triathlon, experienced many sunsets, and perfected my biscotti recipe. I've reconnected with old relationships and made many new friends. I got caught in ice storms on mountain peaks in New Zealand, was bit by strange bugs in the Guatemalan rain forest, and haven't had to restock on panty hose yet. I got out and did a lot of the things I fantasized about in my old gray cubicle. I had a plan, a vision, a driving force that I could create my own job description, a smorgasbord of creativity and personal passions. I proved that I didn't have to simply accept the corporate destiny card I had been handed.

YOU'RE NOT ALONE

There are increasing numbers of people in our generation, people in their twenties and thirties, who are struggling with career and life issues and are opting to check out of the corporate world.

- Only 1 percent of 1,000 adults recently surveyed about career preferences said they want to be corporate managers.
- Approximately 10 percent of Americans ages twenty-five to thirty-four are actively working on starting a business, a rate three times higher than any other age group.

(*Fortune*, 2/20/95 and *Forbes*, 5/8/95)

Meet some people who are in various stages of kissing off corporate America. You'll meet them in more detail later in the book, but here's a quick introduction:

Dave gave himself a unique Christmas present last year: He quit his job. Having worked in engineering since college, he was "bored out of my mind," he admitted over a latte at one of our coffeehouse bull sessions. He knew there was something out there but wasn't quite sure what. When he thinks back, his happiest times were those spent working with his hands. His initial thoughts on next steps include exploring starting his own home renovation business, possibly through an apprenticeship. But he's worried about how he'll pay the rent through this transition process.

Terri likes to play the corporate game—sometimes. And only when she wants to. She worked in corporate marketing for several years after school, and then decided it was time to hit the world of self-employment. Now she runs her own successful temp business through which she hires herself out to various corporations that need someone for either a short time or on a retainer basis. She thinks she has the best of both worlds, especially now that her son is one year old. She's looking for ways to continue to balance her roles as entrepreneur and mom.

Annie is struggling. She has a very cushy, comfy job at a large bank. The job has its moments but more downs than ups. She knows this isn't the right place for her in the long term, but it's getting very comfortable. If she stays a couple more years, she'll become a partner, and profit-sharing will kick in. That is, if she doesn't go crazy before then. She knows she needs motivation, support, advice, and some tools to get started.

You are probably at some stage of kissing off corporate America as you read this book. You may have already kissed off and jumped full force into a new venture. Or you may have kissed off and are floundering in a bit of gray limbo, trying to nail down what is next for you. Maybe you've been down on the corporate scene for a while, but you're not sure about kissing off. Whatever your background or current situation, remember you're not alone. You'll be meeting other people informally throughout this book who share their experience and advice.

LOCT—"LIFE OUTSIDE THE CORPORATE TRACK"

In different ways, we are all searching for our own personal LOCT: a Life Outside the Corporate Track. This can and should mean different things to different people, but it is comprised of similar elements.

Life

The corporate world will typically take away control of your life. Your independence and freedom may go down the tubes or be relegated to an occasional Saturday and Sunday evening. In LOCT, a renewed value is placed on all aspects of life, of enjoying and living life to the fullest, taking advantage of serendipitous picnics, naps, and deep conversations around campfires.

Creativity

Think outside the norm. Be innovative. Be creative. Break down the status quo—accepted notions of "careers" and write your own definitions and expectations. Envision a life where the traditional concepts of work and life are more interchangeable and interrelated. Break out of the box.

WHY BUST OUT NOW?

Why should you contemplate making such a career jump now? You probably hear the voices of well-intentioned friends and family in the background chorus, with your mother or father as lead vocalist, singing refrains like:

- The economy is bad. Why leave a good job?
- Why did you go to college?
- You don't have enough experience.
- How will you pay the rent/pay off student loans/feed the cat?
- What will I tell the neighbors?
- Aren't you ever going to get married, buy a house, have kids, water the plants?
- Isn't it about time you started taking life seriously?
- You're going to regret this, you know. . . .

Believe me, I've heard it all. And it's a powerful, convincing song, perhaps because it often comes from people

> "I'm a young female marketing/communications professional, and I think I'm not alone in my feelings of being a yuppie/Gen X castaway. I have a drive to work all night, and make a ton of money, and drive a Lexus. The other side of me screams for a simple life of not living in the rat race, making a living baking bagels and living in the country."
> —Posted in the "Quit the Rat Race" folder on America OnLine

very close to us whom we love. Change is hard. Looking at life from a new perspective is hard. It's hard to look people you love in the eye and say, "I hear what you're saying, but I disagree. I have to do what's right for me."

When I told my parents I was quitting my advertising job, backpacking through Australia for two months with my boyfriend, then coming back to do "something else" (not a detailed job description, I admit), I could barely choke out the sentence. I knew they would disapprove. I knew they wouldn't understand and would be disappointed. I was veering off the path they had envisioned for me, the one where I marry a successful accountant and we move into a glossy suburban town house with two Saabs in the garage.

It's a tough situation because at a time in your life when you need the utmost in support and warm fuzzies, important people in your life may bail. We'll talk more about dealing with pressures from family and friends later on in chapter 7.

So why is our generation crazy enough to kiss off the corporate world? What is driving us to say "thanks but no thanks" to blue suits and cubicles? Here are some thought-starters.

We've Learned from the Yuppies of the '80s

We've learned a lot of lessons by growing up in the 1980s. We watched the yuppies rise and burn out; we've seen them get caught up in the trap of materialism and consumerism. We've substituted mountain bikes for their BMWs, backpacks for Club Meds.

We've seen the dual-career couple of the 1980s caught in a vicious cycle of day care, guilt, and exhaustion. We know we need to create a balanced lifestyle. We can appre-

From "Generation X" to the "post-boomers," our generation has been described with more labels than Campbell's soup cans. One perk to this is there has been a lot of analysis written on our generation. For some varying perspectives, sample:

Bill Strauss and Neil Howe, (Vintage Books, 1993)

13th Gen

This book is sort of the granddaddy of the Gen X analysis books. Although written by two boomers, the book is filled with easy-to-digest statistics and analysis on the roots of what made our generation what it is today.

David Lipsky and Alexander Abrams, (Times Books, 1994)

Late Bloomers: Coming of Age in Today's America.

The Right Place at the Wrong Time

Similar to *13th Gen*, this book is an analysis and critique of post-boomers in the context of today's economic and political climate.

Geoffrey T. Holtz, (St. Martin's Press, 1995)

Welcome to the Jungle:

The Why Behind Generation X

Another perspective on why our generation is the way it is, well researched with lots of statistics.

Michael Lee Cohen, (Plume, 1994)

The Twenty-something American Dream:

A Cross-Country Quest for a Generation

Talk about a dream job. Cohen received a grant to travel the country, interviewing people in their twenties from a variety of social and economic backgrounds, the results of which form this book.

ciate the niceties of life, but we know not to make that the end goal.

Now Is the Time to Experiment

This doesn't mean we don't have any responsibilities. Many of us do have mortgages, kids, spouses. Others are rapidly advancing toward the commitment of owning a houseplant. We'll talk more about organizing and balancing marriages, family, and children in chapter 7. Still, if we are ever to kiss off, this is our time to experiment, to climb out on a limb, to take a chance.

We Are Not Cookie-Cutter Corporate Clones (Yet)

The warning signs of becoming a cookie-cutter corporate clone: Your memos all have the same opening phrase: "The purpose of this memo is. . . ." You ride the same bus at the same time and sit in the same seat every day. Every so often a crazy, colorful idea shoots through your brain and your reaction is, "Maybe someday, when I have the time."

Cookie-Cutter Corporate Clone: Those working in the corporate environment who tend to look alike, cut from the same mold. The clones thrive in the corporate workplace where employees and ideas are all identical, with no sense of newness or creativity.

We're a generation that is growing old before our time. We all have creative souls inside us that are getting lost in the corporate labyrinth. Think back to the treehouse you engineered at age six, your role in the junior-high school play, things that came to you naturally, given the right environment. If you feel your creativity being stifled by traditional work constraints, now is the time to make some changes before you lose touch completely.

Lead the Corporate Workplace Revolution!

The corporate security blanket is in tatters. We post-boomers realize that, but are we doing anything about it? We know that the lifelong job that Dad had at IBM is no more (and would we want it anyway?).

Self-employment is on the rise. Working at home is on

ANGELA, AGE 24, HOUSTON

"I think our generation views the concept of a career much differently than the yuppies of the 1980s did. We don't want to separate our work from the rest of our lives—we see things more integrated. I don't feel like my job should be something I do just to earn money so I can do what I really want to during the weekend. Life is too short for that, and I don't want to end up having this major midlife crisis because I never followed my true passions and my real dreams. I don't have any passion for the job I have right now in brand management. I've been feeling this way for the last couple of months. I know I can't stay here long-term, but I've been so crazed at work that I just don't have time to think about what's next or what's right for me."

> "The Information Age has arrived. In the years ahead, new, more sophisticated software technologies are going to bring civilization ever closer to a near-worker-less world. In the agricultural, manufacturing, and service sectors, machines are quickly replacing human labor and promise an economy of near-automated production by the mid-decades of the twenty-first century."
> —Jeremy Rifkin, *The End of Work: The Decline of the Global Labor Force and the Dawn of the Post-Market Era* (Putnam, 1995)

the rise. Telecommuting and the home office are blossoming, thanks to the growth of mass-accessible technology such as fax machines, the Internet, laptops, modems, and elaborate home phone systems. This works to our generation's advantage as we grew up on the cutting edge of technology and we easily rely on and incorporate it into all aspects of our lives. Think about it: We really are the first generation to have such access to the tools that make busting off the corporate path achievable.

What this means is that one's "work" is growing more self-defined. There are more options available to express yourself. For example, you can set up a professional home office that enables you to start many types of businesses relatively quickly and at minimal cost. The traditional work world is being replaced due to these new tools. Many more options and opportunities are available for our generation.

MYTHS ABOUT BUSTING

Before we go any further, let's clear up some myths about busting off the corporate track. These myths are often the knee-jerk responses you get when you first run the idea through your mind. They may be in the form of doubts brewing around in the back of your mind, slowly chewing away at your self-confidence or causing you to question yourself and your commitment to kissing off.

Myth No. 1: Corporate Life Is Evil

No. And I'm not saying that to elude the wrath of the millions of corporate employees of the world. Or to leave myself the out of someday getting my old job back. I was serious when I said that I don't regret my corporate stint, and if I had to do it over, I wouldn't do it any other way. I just couldn't stay there.

Corporate life can be a great jungle gym of learning and opportunities. Take advantage of it while you're there. For me, it was a very necessary first step into the "real world." The question for many of us is when is it time for that experience to end and a new, different adventure to begin.

Some of us are perfectly cut out for the corporate-life mold, and that's fine. We all know someone who fits perfectly into the corporate glove and whose life appears always rosy. It's hard not to compare ourselves with these people and wonder why we can't be blissful in our cubicle. Hard to say. They may have the traditional life crisis at fifty. They may be scared to really question themselves. Don't bother overanalyzing and don't waste time criticizing. We have enough work to do on our own.

Obviously, I'm not saying that corporations should be

abolished. Traditional, large corporations today form the backbone of the American economy. They produce goods and jobs, and they contribute to our overall standard of living. Most of us leaving corporate America are doing so not primarily because of institution size but rather the stagnant mentality that too often brews within. It is the bureaucratic philosophy that needs to be reexamined and reengineered, which won't be accomplished simply by doing away with the Fortune 500.

When I told my dad the title of this book, he jumped to accuse me of being "anti-American." In his eyes, I was arguing to abolish everything that made America what it is today. In my eyes, this new work revolution hearkens to the original tenets on which this country was founded: individualism, questioning and breaking away from the status quo, and a movement toward self-sufficiency. We're the pioneers of the 1990s, changing forever the boundaries and definitions of work.

Myth No. 2: This Change Will Be Easy

Well, yes and no. Change is rarely "easy." Taking that step into your boss's office to hand in a resignation letter and tell her you're working freelance is no picnic. But if you are following your heart, if you are doing what you know is right for you, the pieces will fall into place. Doing what I and so many others have done isn't easy; I was plagued by self-doubt, worry, guilt—you name it, I felt it. I still sometimes wake up overwhelmed with the feeling of "who am I and what the hell do I think I'm doing?" But there has always been something inside me that pushes me forward. While I'm often scared where I'm standing, I have no desire to take a step back.

> "There is a vitality, a life-force, an energy, a quickening that is translated through you into action and because there is only one of you in all of time, this expression is unique. And if you block it, it will never exist through any other medium and be lost."
>
> —Martha Graham

This book is designed to serve as a catalyst toward your change. Through the sharing of ideas and the personal experiences of many, we're creating a sort of virtual support network. The better we understand what we're feeling and experiencing, the better we can grasp and tackle change.

Myth No. 3: You Must Become an Entrepreneur

No, you don't have to rush out, hang up your shingle, and start a business according to an MBA format. But you do have to always *think* entrepreneurially. Creatively. Artistically. Bring new perspectives to the plate.

Innovation is a theme running throughout this book. It is the lifelong philosophy of breaking down old paradigms and looking at things from a new point of view. You're doing that already just by reading this and starting to reevaluate your work situation. We'll be touching back on the innovation and entrepreneurial theme, giving more practical suggestions and ideas.

Myth No. 4: You Will Starve

Remember Ramen Noodles? Those dry noodles that cost next to nothing for next-to-nothing taste that fueled you through college? Better rekindle your nostalgia. No, I'm not saying you will be dirt poor or, worse yet, go into credit card hell. What I am saying is that you have to truly want this change and be willing to make the financial and emotional commitment. You can't bust off the corporate path by day and talk about it over trendy microbrews by night on your American Express gold card.

I'm talking about passionate, unswerving commitment. It's one thing to read about kissing off. It's one thing to talk about, even to develop, a plan of attack. It becomes real when you take action, when you put the pedal to the metal and drive. You must want this so badly, have your end goal so clear in your mind, that you're willing to sacrifice what previously had seemed so important.

JOHN, AGE 29, CINCINNATI

John is a former advertising account executive now involved with the start-up of a coffee-drink company. He says: "I remember the day I realized that the ad agency life might not be a long-term job for me. I asked my boss, who had recently been promoted to executive vice president, how he liked the new high-level, corner office job. 'It's nice,' he said. 'Indoor job, no heavy lifting.' Yeah, he was being rather sarcastic, but it made me realize that there were those people who found 'no heavy lifting' to be a benefit. And there were those of us who prefer getting our hands dirty. College is supposed to expand your options but often ends up creating a tunnel vision. Perhaps one reason I like my new job so much is that I do have to lift boxes from time to time, or spend days pushing latte samples in the park."

BUSTING RULES

These probably shouldn't be called "rules." Too restrictive. Think of them as guidelines—suggestions—"things I wish I knew before." Expanded in detail later on, here are some general ideas to start thinking about.

Seek Out a Support Network

Now that you've made the decision to make some major life changes, before you go any further, before you read or do anything else, ask yourself: Who is the one person in this world who would react with a big "That's terrific. What can I do to help?" This book is designed to be one source of support, but it's important to seek out people who can keep you motivated, inspired, and kicking.

Warning No. 1: It probably won't be your parents and family. They want to protect us, and cozy corporate cubicles operate under the pretense of exactly that. Parents and family mean well, but security and stability will most likely be their number one priority for you. This type of change will knock them for a loop, and their reaction could be severe, which is not what you need at this point.

Warning No. 2: Don't be surprised if you get snide, at times cutting, reactions from old friends. What they are really saying is "I wish I could do what you're doing but I don't have the guts and I'm jealous." It's a shame, really, but all you can do is smile, bite your tongue, and go on. So when you choose that friend who will help you through all this, sit her down and let it all out. Tell her you're scared. Tell her you're confused. Tell her you're not exactly sure what needs to happen, but you know something does. Then tell her that she has full authority to kick your butt at any and all times. Period. Trust me, you'll need it. Make sure the system is in place.

Warning No. 3: Societally, what you are contemplating, and in the end doing, is breaking new ground. Yes, self-employment, home offices, nonsuit work attire, and working hours other than nine to five are growing in acceptance. But these work styles are still perceived as alternative. As was true when I left the agency, today I spend a lot of my time educating colleagues, clients, and vendors about what I'm doing and how I'm doing it. Often I have to fight to be treated professionally. Just because you've set out on this new path doesn't mean the world in general will be wholly responsive. Establish relationships with key people in your new endeavors. Get to know your FedEx driver and the Kinko's copy staff. These people are the buster's support staff.

Keep Taking Small Bites

Don't let all this overwhelm you. I often made that mistake when I first started developing my LOCT. After I made the serious decision to leave corporate life, I spent too many evenings numb from anxiety over everything I had to do. I felt that once I made the decision, I had to do it all, today. Figure out my life, write a business plan, write a book, travel around the world, today. Don't let that get to you. Take things slowly. Prioritize. Focus.

Don't set up frustrating traps for yourself before you start by creating unrealistic expectations. This process takes, and should take, time—maybe a couple of years. More

> "One can begin to reshape the land-scape with a single flower."
> —Spock, *Star Trek*

about planning specifics in chapter 3, but for now, don't be too hard on yourself, and don't get caught up in overly complicated decisions. For starters, simply focus on doing one thing right now; it's amazing how little steps lead to big leaps.

2

Trash the Word "Job"

"I Don't Want to Be a Cookie-cutter Corporate Clone"

When I was a kid, I was into *Little House on the Prairie*—the books and the TV series. I even did my best Laura Ingalls imitation one year for Halloween. Looking back, I think it was the "pioneer" job description that really sparked my inner passions. I fantasized about cruising in a covered wagon, blazing the trail to new worlds.

In a way, today we are all pioneers of the 1990s workplace. The home office. Computer technology. Changing rules of business. Growth of the Internet. Vanishing corporate security. "Dressing down" khaki office ensembles from the Gap. These all represent the new workplace territory. The rules are changing, and we are the first generation to leap full force into the possibilities.

WE'RE NOT BABY BOOMERS

The media analyzes and reanalyzes our generation, trying to label us and fit all 40 million of us into a nice, neat niche for the research department. Are we apathetic? Grungy? Lazy? Or hardworking? Entrepreneurial? Socially conscious? The bottom line is we don't fit into one simple box definition. We don't fit in a box because we're as complex as any generation; we're evolving, changing.

We've been stereotyped as the generation that prioritizes play over work, the antithesis of the ambitious, hardwork-

---

Our generation has experienced more than our fair share of labels, covering all extremes:

"The Gen X hucksters: Are these self-styled young pundits out to save an America in decline—or just to get on some cool talk shows?"

—*New York* (8/28/94)

"Grunge and Grit: Don't underestimate Generation X—the most entrepreneurial youngsters yet."

—*Forbes* (5/8/95)

"Move over, Boomers. The Busters are here—and they're angry."

—*Business Week* (12/14/92)

"The Youth Movement: Slackers, schmackers. Gen X bosses put their stamp on business."

—*U.S. News & World Report* (9/23/96)

ing, corporate go-getters of the baby boomers. In truth, we simply have a different vision for our future, a vision that encompasses creativity, imagination, balance. I call it your "life pursuit." It's the idea that all elements of your life are important and need to be continually developed and balanced.

"But are you saying anything new?" you ask. Aren't the bookstore shelves already stacked with New Age–type books that the baby boomers are buying up? Books on leading a balanced life? Simplifying your life? Frugality?

Yes, but the difference is that the boomers have lived over half their lives and are only beginning to realize this. The boomers built their lives around a corporate model and then found out that it is restrictive and unfulfilling. Our generation knows in advance that the concept of embracing a bureaucratic office environment was not designed to enrich one's health, intellectual stimulation, or mental challenge.

Now, midstream in their careers, boomers are trying to forge a philosophical detour. That's tough because:

> **Life Pursuit:** Defining one's life from a broader, self-created perspective. The idea that life is more than a job description, that all elements of our lives are intertwined and interrelated, that all aspects of life should reflect one's individuality.

"To all you who feel burned out, I can only offer my story. I am forty-five years old. I am in a position I have worked very hard for. I gave it my all. I got as high as I could, in a man's world. Now I am so burned out I do not know if I can pick myself up. My hair is falling out, my blood pressure is bad. I am so tired I cannot think, and just getting through the day is an effort. Keeping up at work has become difficult because I am no longer sharp in my thinking. . . . Get out while you can. The money is not worth it. It will destroy your health. It's too easy for us to burn out."
—Posted in the "Quit the Rat Race" folder on America OnLine

- They have significant financial obligations.
- Their hearts may desire something else, but their minds are trapped in "cubicle think."
- They are entrenched in societal expectations: the nice car, house, espresso machine, and so on.

Our generation is still "fresh." A wee bit green when it comes to life in a cubicle. We have tarried on the corporate fence, but we haven't leaped to the other side. We're looking through a window onto the corporate world and are saying "thanks, but no thanks" while we're still able to experiment and explore the alternatives.

WHY ARE WE LEADING THE "KISS-OFF" REVOLUTION?

Why is this happening to us? Why are we so different? Why do we feel like square pegs being forced into round corporate carrels? The answer could be any or all of the following:

1. We're Techie-Confident

Our grandparents reminisce about their first ride in an automobile. Our parents can recall the day television first entered

Cubicle Think: Keeping all your perspectives within the confines of a small, gray frame of mind. This malaise often occurs after one is deeply entrenched in a regimented, numbing corporate career.

their household. We'll be telling our kids about our first Atari set, or the first time we saw a color computer screen.

We realize the computer is our most valuable tool. We feel comfortable reaching for the restart button, Internet connection, and yes, occasionally, the instruction manual. This extends to cellular phones, pagers, and so on. This techie confidence, or "TC," is pure breakaway power.

The majority of the CEOs of the Fortune 500 aren't TC. Although corporations rely heavily on computers, the broad corporate community has not grasped the unlimited poten-

"After college, as private enterprise began to adopt computer technology in the workplace, Generation X had even better access to new electronic equipment as well as advanced training in software and programming. . . . Boomer managers tended to view computers as word processors or glorified typewriters. . . . Boomers largely failed to perceive the true nature and potential of computers, they literally pushed technology off on the next generation and, in doing so, sometimes sowed the seeds of their own obsolescence."

—Karen Ritchie, *Marketing to Generation X*
(Lexington Books, 1995)

> "As entrepreneurs, members of Generation X have something special going for them. Just as the early twentieth-century American farm boy became a mechanical whiz by playing with his Model T Ford, so did the entrepreneurial generation become computer literate.
>
> *Forbes*, 5/8/96

tial of technology. Technology is for a subcommittee of a post-boomer committee to look into.

From a wonderfully humorous perspective, the *Dilbert* comic strip exploits management's ineptness toward technology. Our generation relates to Dilbert's predicaments only too well. The big picture (often overlooked by management) shows us that technology is not only here to stay but it is the tool that is empowering our generation to lead the workplace revolution.

2. We're Career Chameleons

Our generation anticipates, even expects, career evolution. Corporate loyalty and job security are fictitious; we're aware of this before our first day on the job. This is a key difference between us and generations past.

Perhaps the computer age is the driving force behind this. Whatever the reason, we expect career change; we expect

Career Chameleons: Those who have the ability to readily and successfully transition between career paths; those who apply universal skills to various job situations.

For a firsthand, personal account of a boomer's plight through corporate downsizing hell, pick up *White-Collar Blues: Management Loyalties in an Age of Corporate Restructuring* (Basic Books, 1995) by Charles Heckscher. It's well written, but be prepared for large doses of cynicism. Author Heckscher epitomizes the boomers' expectation that after dedicating their lives to a corporation they deserve something in return. From a kiss-off perspective, the book can be ironically inspirational.

instability. We're accustomed to chaos. One perk to this eyes-wide-open realization is that perhaps we won't have the midlife, mid-career crises that many fiftysomething executives are having today. Through downsizing and streamlining, upper-management boomers are being pink-slipped before cushy retirement plans kick in. Unfortunately, too many were expecting company loyalty and stability, and they're bitter, as this reality check came too late.

MARK, AGE 26, MADISON

"I was recruited on campus by a large software company to join their research and development department. They gave me the full recruitment speech about how well they treat their employees and how they've never laid anyone off, their great benefits, etc. At the time, all my friends were taking these corporate jobs so I wasn't really thinking about other options—peer pressure, I guess. But I wasn't even at this company for a whole year when they did some major layoffs, and I was let go. It was actually a good thing for me, because I got a couple of months' severance pay, which I used to start planning my landscaping business. Getting fired gave me the push I needed to start my own business."

3. We're the Cynical Generation

No, we're not cynical. Really. We love the way indoor fluorescent lighting engulfs our cubicles, the stimulating intellectual discourse around the water cooler, the warm fuzzies the boss gives every day.

You get the drift. Maybe we're a bit too objective, but we tend to see things for what they're worth. We're not enticed by the engraved pens, watches, and assorted paraphernalia offered as rewards for enduring year after year of corporate life. Corporate rah-rah simply is not our style. Tell it to us straight. Remove the fluff and we can relate.

4. The Elongated Childhood

Answer honestly. When you hear the word *adult,* do you think of yourself or your parents? Though you may have a

> "Once you fly, you will walk with your eyes skyward. For there you have been, and there you will go again."
>
> —Leonardo da Vinci

What the new generation hates:

- The best bureaucrats, and not the best performers, are more likely to get ahead.
- It's too easy to get pigeonholed or stuck in a dead-end job with no way out.
- It takes too long to get enough responsibility, authority, and rewards.
- There's not enough flexibility about where and when you work.
- Top managers say they want risk takers, but they don't.

—*Fortune,* 2/20/95

> **Lifemarker:** Symbolically important event signifying the crossover into another phase or stage of life. Examples: getting married, having children, and buying a house. Lifemarkers can also be personal, representing a turning point of accomplishment in our lives. Examples: paying off a school loan, starting a business, moving to a new city.

house, a spouse, and even—wow—kids, doesn't it feel like our parents are the "adults" and we're still the "kids" drafted to sit at the card table for Thanksgiving dinner?

There's good reason for that. Our generation may go down in history as having the longest adolescence on record. We're crossing a lot of the traditional "lifemarkers" later in life. Statistics show that we're in school longer, marrying later, and buying property later.

The media has often stereotyped our prolonged adolescence as something negative. We've been characterized as "slackers," lazy and apathetic. But you know our generation is far from deserving any of those labels. Crossing these lifemarkers later in life doesn't make us lazy; actually, it's a sign of maturity. By experiencing lifemarkers on our own personal timetable, we're aiming to make smarter, better decisions.

Additionally, crossing lifemarkers later in life has given us the powerful commodity of freedom. The more lifemarkers we cross, the more indebted and obligated we are to other people, the bank, Visa, and so on. Mortgages, marriage, kids, cars. All of these lifemarkers add layers of responsibility to our lives. By not taking on these obligations before we are truly ready, we have more freedom to take on risk. Freedom

> "Since 1970, the average marriage age has crept up from twenty-three to twenty-seven for men and from twenty-one to twenty-five for women."
> —*Time*, 6/9/97

allows us to be more open to options and diverse paths, and to take on new endeavors serendipitously.

THE STARTING LINE

Now that we've explored why we're leading the corporate kiss-off, let's define where you are in the process. As you read this book, you may be at one of the following stages:

Stage 1: Thinking About It

The title *Kiss Off Corporate America* spoke to you from the bookshelf. Your heart responded, "Yes! How?" Lately you've been:

- bitching about work to anyone who will still listen
- lacking motivation and procrastinating (more than usual)
- tired, sleepy, and altogether not yourself
- disgruntled and, bottom line, unhappy

Stage 2: Toes on the Line

You still have all the characteristics of "Thinking About It," but you're starting to take positive action, possibly by:

- organizing your finances to see exactly where you stand
- analyzing your calendar to plan the optimum time to make your break

Stage 3: Over the Border

You've taken the plunge. At this stage, you may:

- have worked till you couldn't take it anymore, quit in a fury with no plan, and you're now simply vegging out and regaining sanity
- be taking some time off to explore new areas and interests for yourself
- be jumping full force into a new venture you've been thinking about for a while

This book is designed to be a resource manual, an offering of ideas and insights for you to use on your journey. Whatever your starting point on this kiss-off adventure, you're in for quite a ride.

> "It is only with the heart that one can see rightly, what is essential is invisible to the eye."
> —Antoine de Saint-Expuéry, *The Little Prince*

WHAT TO PACK FOR THE JOURNEY

Hang tight, the ride is just beginning. You're poised for kissing off, living the LOCT life, leading the charge into the workplace revolution of the next millennium.

Let's now consider the skills you'll need to pack for this journey. I've highlighted some key skills and traits to identify within yourself and strengthen. These abilities are essential to your preparation for this trip off the corporate track.

1. Pack Commitment

Who is the resident whiner among your circle of friends—that person who is always complaining about his or her job, lack of social life, parental problems, financial hole, hair

You know you're ready to bust out when . . .

- *Dilbert* cartoons cover most of the gray on your cubicle walls.
- You avoid answering the "where do you work?" question.
- You've elevated the art of sneaking out early on Fridays to a higher level.
- You know how to make random Internet surfing look like productivity.
- You can recite all the prices from the take-out menu of the deli across the street.

color, love life, whatever? Nothing is right, everything is a problem or crisis. Every pebble on his or her path becomes an immovable boulder.

We've all fallen into the whiner role ourselves from time to time. It's easy to do. It's easier to complain, to hide under a blanket of "woe is me" than it is to take action.

Strip off those self-sympathy sweats you've been lounging in. Time for a reality check: Kissing off corporate America isn't a game you can play halfheartedly and win. Commitment is key. You must be willing to do anything, be anywhere, stand up to anyone to make this work. Commitment means having enough fuel inside you to keep plowing along like the Energizer bunny.

Keeping your commitment level high is not always easy, especially with pressure and advice coming at you from all sides. Here are a few suggestions:

- Identify a public figure who, in your eyes, has "made it." Ideally it will be someone in your field or who shares the same lifestyle as you. Collect magazine articles, photos, whatever you can about this person. Imagine this person giving you a pep talk when needed. Visualize yourself in his or her shoes someday.
- Take care of yourself; tend to mental and physical health. It's hard to be committed when you feel lousy and all you want to do is crawl under the covers. Think of yourself as being in "kiss off" training.
- Read all you can about entrepreneurial thinking. Get inspired. Read all the profile pieces you can find in magazines like *Success*, *Inc.*, and *Entrepreneur*. If they can do it, so can you.

> "It's not the boulder in your path that's the problem. It's the grain of sand in your boot."
> —Anonymous

2. Pack a Willingness to Take Risks

We all have a different perception of what defines *risk*, but basically, it's a willingness to give things a try even when you're not sure of the outcome. To kiss off your job, you'll need to feel comfortable with risky moves. This is a skill you can practice; it's something you get better at the more you do it. Some tactics that will sharpen this skill:

- Tackle your riskiest, scariest tasks first thing in the day. The longer you wait, the higher your anxiety level rises.
- Don't aim for perfection. It's easy to get stuck in an overplanning stage where you keep pondering and analyzing the outcome. Do your homework, and then just do it. Learn as you go. Learn to live with the feeling that a plan or idea is half-baked. Stop tweaking and go with it.

- Keep track of the risks you take. Use your calendar or datebook to jot down the two or three risky things you do each day. Build on each accomplishment.

3. Pack the Ability to Live in the Discomfort Zone

I've always been the person with a plan. Point A led to point B. It was an adjustment for me to start living with uncertainty. It was uncomfortable. But once I started getting used to chaos, I found I like it a lot better than probability and certainty. Predictability grew boring and dull. I find my waking hours much more intense and fulfilling; my days are very long but inspiring.

Living in the discomfort zone means trading the comfort of mundane certainty for the uneasiness of exhilarating uncertainty. Learning to manage amid many variables is an essential skill for this journey.

"The trouble is that the business world is too conservative and fearful of change. All this talk about free enterprise, innovation, entrepreneurship, individuality . . . it's nothing but hot air. High street giants, business empires everywhere, worship mediocrity. In their love affair with giantism they pay public lip service to the need for change, but I believe that unofficially they fear it."

—Anita Roddick, founder of The Body Shop and author of *Body and Soul: Profits with Principles* (Dimensions, 1991)

4. Pack the Ability to Think Outside the Box

When you were a child, did you dream of someday owning an employee ID card from IBM? Of having a closet lined with multiple blue suits? Hard to believe you did. Your days probably were filled with excavating Mom's flower beds for treasure chests hidden by pirates of bygone days. Or coloring murals on the dining-room walls.

In other words, you were creative. You spent your days dreaming and doing, jumping full force into the fancy of the moment. Perhaps Mom was less than thrilled, but overall creativity back then was rewarded.

This creative journey wound down different roads for all of us, but somewhere along the way we hit a roadblock. Our creativity took a detour; outside forces came in, put up orange cones, and steered us down different paths. These outside forces include teachers, parents, and other well-meaning adults, who by their best judgment steered us toward practical career paths.

"Color within the lines" was the refrain of our childhood. In grammar school we became experts at memorizing and regurgitating multiplication tables and battle dates. In high school we dutifully completed the checklist of college entrance to-dos. Practical. Predictable. Secure. Gray flannel. Comfortable.

A healthy dose of practicality is not necessarily evil. You want to be responsible for your life, pay your bills, fill the tank, and fulfill the basic tiers of Maslow. However, over-emphasizing practicality can water down your creative impulses until they are lost so deep within yourself that you forget all about them.

Here's another perspective: Redefine *creativity* as "self-expression." With that in mind, *uncreative* could be defined

> "I never trust someone who can only spell a word one way."
>
> —Andrew Jackson

For some real creativity spark plugs, pick up *Jump Start Your Brain* (Warner Books, 1996) by Doug Hall. A former P&G corporate executive who went through his own kiss-off experience, Hall started his own company to help others, particularly those afflicted with "cubicle think," to expand their creative thinking. The book is filled with how-to exercises and mind games for enhancing creativity.

"Life is like a ten-speed bicycle. Most of us have gears we never use."

—Charles Schulz

as "the expression of others." Creativity, our self-expression, is the link to ourselves, our souls. Consider it the power that fuels our minds, our hearts, and our lives.

Creativity is one of the basic food groups of the spiritual body. Without it, we dry up. Wilt. We are not all that we can be. A creative mind, an alternative perspective, is vital to the LOCT process, as this is our path to success.

5. Pack Your Confident Self-sufficiency

Confident self-sufficiency is the foundation philosophy of the LOCT process: fully believing you can do it. It may

Confident Self-sufficiency: The full belief that you have the ability to make it as a self-employed person. The positive attitude that you can make it on your own. The ability to wing it, fake it, do whatever it takes to go after your entrepreneurial goal.

seem like an overly simple concept, but it's the fuel that will keep you going. Confident self-sufficiency is about being stubborn, not taking no for an answer, not letting the totem poles of conformity stare you down.

TO-DOS WHILE STILL ON THE COMPANY PAYROLL

Whatever your planning persona, here are some things to do while you are still in a corporate situation.

1. Take Advantage of Your Corporate Job

I'm not talking about stealing office supplies. Or company secrets. Or raiding your boss's personnel file. Do consider ways to tangibly improve your skills and, consequently, your self-employment situation. Some ideas:

> "Life is like a movie. Write your own ending, keep believing, keep pretending. We've done just what we set out to do, thanks to the lovers, the dreamers, and you."
>
> —Kermit the Frog

> "Who would have thought the kids would be taking over so soon? Or that they would even want to? They were supposed to be slackers, cynics, drifters. But don't be fooled by their famous pose of repose. Lately, more and more of them are prowling tirelessly for the better deal, hunting down opportunities that will free them from the career imprisonment that confined their parents. They are flocking to technology start-ups, founding small business, and even taking up causes— all in their own way."
>
> —*Time*, 6/9/97

- Decide at what level you want to be when you leave. Is there a certain job title or skill level that will make your corporate skills appear more "real" to the outside? Define what that is and how you can get it.

- Take advantage of any and all training seminars, classes, and so on. Bottom line: They are still free. Keep an eye out for anything related to the Internet and information highway, pertinent topics no matter what your field.

- Identify in-house corporate allies, people at your company with whom you could most likely continue a professional relationship. Who could give you a strong professional recommendation when needed? Who could you go to for advice? This could be your boss, a colleague on the same level, or someone in a different department. Realize who these people are and make solidifying those relationships a key priority while you are still on the inside of the corporate scene. Don't tell them your full LOCT plan just yet. Situation specifics will vary company to company; therefore your best bet is to keep your plan a secret. Information can leak in the strangest ways.

- Start thinking about ways to "sell" your corporate skills when you are self-employed. These modes may or may not be something you want to do long-term, but they may be your quickest ticket to an immediate source of income. Would your company be willing to "hire" you back as an independent contractor after you've left? Are there clients of yours who would be willing to do the same?

- On a practical note, fully utilize your company benefits and perks while you can. Utilize your health benefits; get a physical, dental checkup, or whatever needs to be done. You will have health insurance when you're on your own, so tell your mom not to worry (more on that in chapter 4). But during those first couple of months of self-employment, arguably the first couple of years, regular well visits to the doctor won't be a priority. You may as well take full advantage of whatever policy you currently have.

2. Build a Nest Egg

Ugh. The reality of money. Unless you are inherently wealthy or win the lottery, you need to start thinking about finances. People cross over to self-employment from a variety of financial backgrounds and means. Whatever your resources, insure your success with a money plan.

The importance of having a financial plan can't be stressed enough. The decision you're making is tremendous. You don't want to be forced back into a corporate environ-

AL, AGE 28, MINNEAPOLIS

"Looking back, one thing I wished I had done differently is I really didn't start my first job out of college with any definitive goals. I sort of started my job as a financial analyst with this 'well, let's just see if this works out' attitude. What happened then was, during my fourth year on the job, I grew frustrated and unhappy, and it took me a while to realize I needed a change and what type of change that was. I think if I had started my job with a concrete goal like 'I'm going to stay here for two years, get an account executive title, and then reevaluate,' I could have been a lot more focused, less frustrated, and probably would have started my own business sooner."

ment because you don't have enough money to pay the rent. Why do some people successfully make the financial transition into self-employment while others don't? The key is attitude. Your life pursuit, your self-employment goals, your dream of living the life you want must be your number one, make-you-feel-tingly-inside obsession. All aspects of your life are affected by this, especially your spending habits.

When you're in the corporate scene, making steady money, spending becomes easy. Slipping into materialism becomes easy. Wanting things you have no need (or space!) for becomes easy. Break that cycle. That cycle isn't working for you, that's why you want out. Start now, before you buy another Starbucks grande decaf skim latte.

WHERE ARE WE?

We've officially kicked off the journey. You know you want to lead the LOCT life. Your bags are packed and you're sitting at the station. The question now is, where are you going? Where is this self-employed journey going to lead you? What is your destination? Don't bang your head against the wall because you can't find one magical, ultimate answer. In the self-employed life, there are multiple paths, multiple journeys to take simultaneously. In these next chapters, we'll start exploring these different routes, these various approaches to self-employment, and talk about some of the pragmatic details behind making it happen. So keep your mind open to new ideas and perspectives and keep moving along. Trashing the word *job* takes some foresight and planning. It's not a good idea to leave in a huff or on impulse. So before you kiss off, think about where you're going and what you'll need to take with you.

Read *Your Money or Your Life: Transferring Your Relationship With Money and Achieving Financial Independence* (Penguin, 1993) by Joe Dominguez and Vicki Robin. This book takes you through a hands-on analysis of where your money goes and an understanding of what your "net worth" is. But more important, the book articulates the philosophy of self-sufficiency, of not letting money control your life and your dreams. It also describes how to achieve financial independence. It has become the '90s bible of frugality, tightwads, and simple living, with good reason.

3

The Multiple Layers of Getting Ready for Self-Employment

"If Only I Knew How to Get to Where I Want to Be"

There is a scene in *The Wizard of Oz* where the Scarecrow bewilders Dorothy by telling her that the yellow brick road heads in two different directions, and each is an equally good path to take. Dorothy can't choose—this one? That one? This one? That one? You may be feeling a lot like Dorothy lately with not two, but thousands of possible roads to choose from.

Sure, when you're trapped inside your cubicle, it's easy to fantasize about all the things you'd do if you had the chance. Well, here's your chance—so what's keeping you there? Only kidding—no one expects you to break away so fast; this is only chapter 3. So don't feel bad when you show up for work again tomorrow morning. Too many options keep lots of young professionals stuck on the starting line, feeling too confused to do anything. Hey, even the Scarecrow had a lot of convincing to do before Dorothy agreed to take the path leading into the woods. Before you leave your job behind, make sure you know where you're going and how you intend to get there.

The key is to start somewhere. Here is that place. Whether you feel that you don't have any doable ideas in your head at all, or you're overloaded with multiple ideas, simply start from where you are. Take a deep breath and don't panic, or feel overwhelmed, or bury this book far under the bed. Start your venture away from the corporate world by organizing your thinking around these three preparatory states:

1. **Pay-the-Rent Dreamfunders:** what you will do part-time for bread-and-butter money while you're gearing up for what you really want to do.
2. **Stepping-Stones:** the steps that will lead you to what you really want to do.
3. **Mindfeeds:** what you'll do to stay on top of things and continually focus on learning and personal development.

The rest of this chapter will take a look at the details of each of these. Once you have a handle on how you'll fit each one into your life, you'll be much closer to kissing-off time.

PAY-THE-RENT DREAMFUNDERS

Your dreamfunder should be something you can do part-
time to make quick money and pay the bills while you put
most of your time and energy into working on your long-

JIM, AGE 28, ATLANTA

Mention the word *bar* to twentysomething lawyers, and a flashback of test-taking terror will flash across their faces. Mention the word *bar* to Jim, and he'll point you to his dreamfunder: He's working nights as a bartender as he's establishing his solo legal practice during the day.

Jim moved to Atlanta after law school to start a prestigious fast-tracked position at a leading legal firm. "While the job had all the perks of the corporate world, including a cushy salary and royal benefits, after a year I knew this was not for me. I wasn't practicing 'law' as a tool to help people; I was shuffling papers to rack up billable hours to make money off a big business client."

Realizing he needed to be calling his own shots, Jim left the law firm to set up his own shop. "I want to help other entrepreneurs, provide legal advice and expertise for other people doing the self-employed thing," says Jim. Knowing that this endeavor would take time to be profitable, he quickly found a dreamfunder job as a bartender. "I bartended through law school, so I could easily fall back into it," he says. He works at a downtown bar where the clientele tends to be upscale, ordering pricey hip drinks and leaving bigger tips.

"Aside from paying my rent, bartending ironically keeps me focused and motivated toward establishing my own practice," comments Jim. "Every night I serve a lot of the same type of people: overworked, stressed out, unhappy professionals. Whenever I tell them that I quit to do my own thing, they look at me in awe because they admit they want to do that but don't have the guts. The people at the bar remind me of why I left and what I don't want to become—this keeps me going."

term dreams. This isn't the get-rich-quick part; this isn't about contributing to your investment stock portfolio. This is about earning the money you need to pay your bills. Here is where you might look into franchises and chains who offer surprisingly decent pay, benefits, and perks. Here is where you might regress back to college jobs like restaurant work, tutoring, baby-sitting, housecleaning. Here is where you aren't looking to climb a career ladder; you just want quick money.

When you're looking for a dreamfunder job consider these factors:

- **Flexibility:** Look for something that offers the most flexible work schedule. Remember, you want to have the freedom to act on opportunities related to your big picture as they come up.
- **Consistency:** The goal of a dreamfunder job is to bring in the bread-and-butter money while you make the transition to life outside the cubicle—so you need a constant source of income. Consistency will keep you from stressing over next month's rent or mortgage and allow you to focus on your goals.
- **Payoff:** Don't agonize over finding just the right transition job. It's your time that's most valuable right now, so look for the job that gives you the most money in the least amount of time. The bottom line is cash in your pocket. (Don't forget to factor in your commuting time and expenses.)
- **Fringe benefits:** There are some key perks to look for in your part-time job. Many hourly franchises do give their employees decent health benefits (more on health insurance options in chapter 5). And if you're lucky, your new job will give you contacts and information

> "Champions aren't made in gyms. Champions are made from something they have deep inside them—a desire, a dream, a vision. They have to have last-minute stamina, they have to be a little faster, they have to have the skill and the will. But the will must be stronger than the skill."
>
> —Muhammad Ali

you can use to meet your long-term cash flow goal. Look for work that will give you benefits in training, information, skills, and contacts.

Finding a Dreamfunder

When you're looking for the job that will transition you out of the corporation, think out of the box. Be creative. Talk to everyone to find leads. Get the word out that you're looking for part-time work with a flexible schedule. Contact chapters of various associations. Attend meetings and network. Find people who are building new companies and can't afford full-time employees just yet. Print up flyers and post them at train stations, and libraries, and put them on cars in the faculty parking lots of local colleges. And don't overlook the obvious—check the classified ads.

This isn't a good time to settle for just anything that gets you out of the nine-to-five rat race. Take your time to find something that will bring in the money and give you time to work toward your dream. Remember: There's no rush, so look before you leap.

DAVE, AGE 30, ORLANDO

"I've always loved bookstores; I just never imagined I'd be working in one." Then again, Dave, a former investment banker, never thought he'd be pursuing his long-lost dream of becoming a writer.

Dave's path off the corporate track is a bit different than many because he didn't choose it. "I was laid off. It was one of those blessings in disguise, though, because I had been so down on my job the last couple of months. I just wasn't at all into what I was doing; I didn't care whether the Dow was heading up or down. I was always doing some writing on the side, but I had never fully focused myself. I saw this pink slip as an opportunity to give my writing a chance."

Dave would get some severance pay from his old job, but he knew he needed more time to really pursue his writing, so he started working at his favorite local bookstore. "I sort of did it on a whim. I was poking around there on a Saturday afternoon, as I often do, and I saw the 'Help Wanted' sign, applied, and got the job."

At the time, Dave didn't fully realize the positive impact working at the bookstore would have on his writing career. Overall, just being in a literary environment was inspiring and made this new direction feel real. The bookstore dreamfunder job not only helped pay the bills, but it gave Dave an opportunity to pragmatically start learning about the writing business. "As I assisted customers in the store, I could ask questions about what they liked to read and why they chose a particular book. I could also chat with the publishers' sales reps that came into the store and learn about what made a book sellable." Dave's dreamfunder was feeding his dream in more ways than one.

Dreamfunder Roadblocks

"Quick buck" jobs are your ticket to freedom, but if you're not careful they can entangle you in their own kind of web. Watch out for these traps:

The Hamster Wheel. You've seen hamsters run and run for hours on those little wheels that go nowhere. Your transition job shouldn't turn you into one of these hamsters. If you work so hard and run so fast to pay your basic bills, all your other dreams, visions, and plans can fall to the wayside. When you become tired, frustrated, and unhappy, the stable and secure work in the corporate world will start looking very appealing again. If a corporate job is dangled in

KAREN, AGE 26, CHICAGO

"Don't overlook traditional job-search outlets for your dreamfunder. I found mine in the newspaper classifieds. I knew I needed to get out of working in an ad agency, but for me the problem wasn't really what I was doing, but rather the environment I was in. I enjoyed the marketing aspects; it was the twelve-hour days and total lack of control over my schedule that were driving me insane. I found a part-time job in the Sunday job section as a promotion coordinator. This New York–based company needed someone local in Chicago part-time to manage some regional events and promotions, but it wasn't enough work to justify a full-time position. That worked out fine by me because it gave me income to pay the rent, yet I still had flexibility and time to explore other things. This company was happy to find someone with my expertise and background who wanted something part time. Most people applying for the spot were recent graduates without experience who were willing to take any job they could find."

> "To keep our faces toward change and behave like free spirits in the presence of fate is strength undefeatable."
>
> —Helen Keller

front of you, you're very likely to take it. You may be satisfied for a little while (anything is better than that hamster wheel), but you'll slowly come back around to where you started.

Temp Work. Avoid getting your dreamfunder job through a temp agency unless they can offer you flexible hours and scheduling. When you get stuck in jobs doing mindless work from nine to five, in addition to the hassle of dressing for work and commuting, your brain switches gears and your creativity slumps. You'll have no time or energy to focus on your next steps, and you're back on the hamster wheel.

The Money Pit. We're our own worst enemy sometimes. We claim we want to leave the corporate circuit, so we quit our job and find a dreamfunder transitional job. However, we continue to live as though we're on a corporate salary. We charge the latest CDs, order pricey take-out food for dinner, and go out with friends for drinks. Do the math: It won't work. Initially, you must be willing to make sacrifices to reach your goal. Kissing off corporate America is more than a career tweak. It's a significant lifestyle recasting that requires dedication. So before you leap, ask yourself if this is truly the right time for you to see this through 100 percent. Can you and do you genuinely want to see this through?

Peer Pressure. It feels great thinking about kissing off, but how will you feel when you're serving a double mocha at Starbucks to someone from the old office? It isn't easy. You have to be committed. You have to want this intensely. And you have to be willing to disregard the pangs of peer pressure. I have to admit, it has taken me a long time. I used to downplay some of the things I did initially to make money.

LYDIA, AGE 32, NEW YORK

"Looking back, I was so eager to get out of my cubicle and try something new that I jumped without a plan," admits Lydia, a computer consultant. "I was feeling so disconnected and frustrated with my engineering job and the New York City lifestyle that I started fantasizing over doing something that would be meaningful, something through which I could make a positive impact, a difference. So when my lease expired, I quit my job, packed up my stuff, and moved to Washington, D.C., with the idea that I would do something in public service, maybe in politics or at a governmental agency."

But things didn't go as smoothly as planned. "I quickly got a job at a temp agency doing mindless clerical stuff. I thought that this would be an easy way to pay the rent, but the job was pretty much nine to five, which left me little time to do any networking or job searching. Plus, the cost of living is pretty high in D.C., so I constantly felt behind."

After a year, Lydia moved back with her family in New Jersey and took a job as a computer consultant for a small company. "I learned a lot from my D.C. stint, but it mostly was experience in what not to do. I know now you can't jump out of a secure corporate gig without a plan, especially a financial plan. I'll probably be at my job now for a while to save some money and figure out what my next steps will be."

I avoided discussing it with people who would make me feel insecure about my decision. But I wouldn't let peer pressure ruin my dreams. Over time it becomes easier. Once you start moving from short-term dreamfunder pay-the-bills jobs into your long-term, this-is-what-I-really-want-to-be-doing agenda, your confidence and esteem will grow proportionally with your passion and enthusiasm. When you realize you are actively moving forward with your big-picture life and plans, your focus will become clear because you can see something greater, something pivotal, straight ahead. (Further information on handling the people in your life and creating support structures is included in chapter 7.)

STEPPING-STONES

Stepping-stones are an assortment of income-generating activities, all going on at the same time, that lead you to where you want to be. This is the foundation of your dream—the route you will take to get to your goal.

There can be several layers of stepping-stones that keep a variety of projects on your plate. These may overlap, be extensions of one another, or be related in many other ways, but they all have strong big-picture potential. This multilevel approach has a number of benefits. First, you're diversifying your income sources, leading to greater long-term financial stability. Think of it along the lines of a well–thought out, diverse stock portfolio. By investing your time and energy in a variety of activities versus one exclusively, you're increasing your overall, long-term rate of return. If one doesn't pan out or bring in the planned income, you've got other things going on that will keep you afloat.

The layering approach also adds a continual jolt of creativity and innovation to your LOCT lifestyle. Alternating between projects creates a synergy, a connection that fosters creativity and inspires new visions and ideas. Life on the stepping-stones may seem a bit unbalanced, chaotic, and tumultuous at times, but it's also invigorating, stimulating, and inspiring.

There are literally thousands of stepping-stones you can travel along that will lead you to your ultimate goal, but most of them fall within the following three categories. Think of these three as mere suggestions to initiate brainstorming for your own income-generating opportunities. These are not strict rules to follow; they are offered only to get your brain thinking innovatively.

Creation

Creation is commerce in its most basic form: You produce an item and sell it. This item can be something you craft by hand such as earrings, clothing items, cabinet woodwork, or flower arrangements. Creation can mean inventing a unique prototype for mass production such as jewelry, bike accessories, T-shirts, or hair accessories. It may mean cutting your own CD or self-publishing a collection of your best recipes. Or you may purchase an item, add to or enhance it, and then package it for resale. This could include furniture refinishing, antique restoration, or rebuilding classic cars. Wherever your dream is taking you, think creatively about what you can produce or create to lead you there.

Resource Access

On this stepping-stone, you can look around at your available tools and resources and think of ways they can help you generate income while pulling you closer to your goal. Take your camera, for instance. If you want to be a writer, offer pictures to go along with your stories and you'll increase sales and raise the fee you can charge. If you want to go into catering and happen to be talented with a camera, you can rent top-notch equipment, get into the wedding photo business, and learn loads about wedding catering. If you want to go into the home renovation business, use your power tools to start a small handy/repair service. If the computer is your thing, use it to network by setting up web pages for potential clients or graphic design materials for future customers. Use what you have to get what you want.

Service Provider

This stepping-stone lets you get paid for what's in your head, and there are lots of ways to do this. You can journey closer to your goal by selling your expertise on a per-project basis and calling yourself a consultant. You can boost your income and your status as an expert by creating and selling a newsletter or by writing columns for various publications. How about teaching? Contact community colleges, evening extension programs, and adult education centers and offer to instruct classes. Or you can offer your services as a tutor, where clients pay you on an hourly basis. You might also consider public speaking engagements on your area of expertise. You can offer a workshop, seminar, or lecture through the library system, you can set up your own presentation and charge participants, or you can speak for free simply to generate publicity for yourself and your idea. Anytime you share what you know, you learn more about it yourself and you meet people who may be helpful to you down the road.

MINDFEED

All our lives, our education has been narrow and channeled. Most of us went from elementary school to junior high or middle school to high school to college to a job. Assistant account executive to account executive to supervisor. Precalculus to calculus. Brownies to Girl Scouts. On this educational, straight-ahead track we didn't have a chance to truly think about our personal needs and choose a path of knowledge best for us.

Mindfeeds to the rescue. This is a piece of your breakaway plan that focuses on your personal quest for knowl-

Are you contemplating your big idea? Trying to figure out your passion, your driving interest? There are a number of engaging, helpful books available to help you organize and develop your dreams and visions.

Laurence G. Boldt, (Penguin, 1993)
Zen and the Art of Making a Living:
A Practical Guide to Creative Career Design
Zen is an innovative, unconventional, yet pragmatic career guide. It includes exercises and worksheets to help you identify the type of work that would be satisfying for you.

Richard Bolles, (Ten Speed Press, 1996)
What Color Is Your Parachute? 1997:
A Practical Manual for Job-Hunters and Career-Changers
This book is the bible of career planning. It focuses on how to find a "traditional" job (i.e., writing your résumé, interview techniques, etc.). However, the book begins with some very effective, thought-provoking writing exercises designed to identify and understand your true passion.

Marsha Sinetar, (St. Martin's Press, 1996)
To Build the Life You Want, Create the Work You Love:
The Spiritual Dimension of Entrepreneuring

Marsha Sinetar, (Dell Books, 1990)
Do What You Love, the Money Will Follow:
Discovering Your Right Livlihood
Author Marsha Sinetar's philosophy is very similar to mine: All aspects of our lives are interconnected and related. A "job" should not be something that compels us to wear a mask from nine to five. Sinetar's books are packed with various self-exploration exercises and strong motivational boosts.

Julia Cameron and Mark Bryan, (JP Tarcher, 1992)

The Artist's Way:

A Spiritual Path to Higher Creativity

This book is not a traditional career guidance book, but it provides a method for connecting with your true self. This book focuses on developing your creativity, and the various exercises and activities in the book are very effective in self-exploration.

Jack V. Matson, (Paradigm Press, Ltd., 1996)

Innovate or Die:

A Personal Perspective on the Art of Innovation

Again, not a traditional career book, but very helpful. Written in an informal tone (to be expected, given the cartoonish dinosaur on the cover), Matson's off-beat approach to failure highlights some of those traps we often fall into. His main philosophy is that "intelligent fast failure" is one of the most effective tools to create, try, test, revamp, or start over with. Fear of failure can be crippling to LOCTs. It prevents progress and stalls our development. Matson's message is to learn quickly from our failure and take that knowledge into our next idea.

edge using a mix of alternative, experiential, and traditional classrooms. While your dreamfunder job is paying the bills and your stepping-stone experiences are generating a bit of income and bringing you closer to the goal, a mindfeed can give you time and distance to think, plan, and ponder how all the pieces fit into the jigsaw puzzle of life. Here you voluntarily put yourself in situations that challenge and enlighten you and bring you closer to having what you want in life.

Mindfeeds incorporate the same overall philosophy and qualities that drive the LOCT lifestyle:

JACK, AGE 27, BOSTON

Jack is a traveler at heart. "I must have some Gypsy in my soul," he says with a grin. Jack dabbled in entrepreneurial endeavors while an undergrad, ranging from producing T-shirts to helping start a restaurant. "But then I got sucked into the corporate system. I had loans to pay, and everyone around me was going out and getting jobs with all the perks, so I just went with the flow," he explains.

After a couple of years on the advertising fast track, he knew he had to jump off. He had been trying to ignore his travel-bug tendencies and wanderlust, but finally gave in and went to India for three months. "The agency I worked for gave me a leave of absence so I could have my job back when I returned. I think they saw this as sort of a pre-midlife crisis and I'd get it out of my system and over with. But I knew from the minute I stepped off the plane that there was something else out there for me."

That "something else" has proven to be several travel-related endeavors. During that India trip, Jack started to refine his photography skills. "I had always considered my photos a hobby, but now I started looking at them as a potential pocket of income that could keep me traveling," he explains. He wrote a personal travel experience essay for a local magazine that also ran some of his photos. "I didn't get paid much for that," says Jack, "but it was a start, my first published credit. My next goal is to try to pitch some ideas to some more national travel magazines, so I might possibly be on a real assignment on my next trip."

Jack's enthusiasm for travel has sparked some other tourism-related entrepreneurial ideas in his head. "I don't think enough people travel to out-of-the-way, developing places like India or Africa. They are perceived as too 'out there' or not safe. I'm working on a business plan for a travel company that would organize trips for the average person to go to these places, that would take the fear and apprehension away and replace it with a sense of wonder and discovery." In the meantime, Jack is working part-time at a local travel agency. "I'm doing pretty basic stuff there, offering the typical gamut of cruises and Caribbean packages. But I'm learning the industry, getting a sense of what people want from their vacation experiences, and I'm paying the rent as I go."

- **The desire for flexibility:** Give me the freedom to pursue topics of my own choice on my own terms.
- **The desire for independence:** Don't tell me what to think; give me an environment where I can think for myself.
- **The desire to be creative:** Teach me ways to express myself, to stimulate my mind to think innovatively.
- **The desire to enhance skills:** Show me how to keep up with our ever-changing world. I need to know how my role is evolving in our mercurial society.

There are many ways you can build a mindfeed. Three general types you might want to investigate are: (1) experiential sabbaticals, (2) experiential travel, and (3) the traditional classroom. These learning options are open to you at any stages of the kiss-off process and on any schedule that fits your needs. You might choose one over the others; you might try one, two, or all three; you might take time off from work to immerse yourself, or you might use a mindfeed as your stepping-stone (keeping in mind that mindfeeds do not generate income—they feed your mind and soul, not your bank account).

As you read through the following descriptions of the three types of mindfeeds, keep your mind open. Let your thoughts flow without censorship. If your mind wanders to thoughts of a jungle expedition, don't shut it down; maybe you're finding your way to volunteering at the local zoo, or taking a course in zoology (or actually traveling to an African jungle—who knows!). Read and welcome all possibilities.

1. Experiential Sabbatical

Do you think about a general field of interest that you'd maybe like to have a future career in but don't know a lot about? Do you want to know more about a topic that isn't covered in a traditional school curriculum because it's so new, specific, or off the wall? Do you feel like you need some time away to think, read, and explore? If it's a yes, think seriously about an experiential sabbatical.

A sabbatical is a study program you design for yourself. It removes you from day-to-day life to let you experience something new. It has no grades and no pressure; the responsibility for learning is all yours. And the places where you can learn are endless. You can begin brainstorming sabbatical ideas around two possibilities.

Volunteering You might decide to volunteer your time to a related cause in your community. Beyond simply showing up to help out a nonprofit group, offer your unique talents to meet your sabbatical needs. You might teach a workshop on a topic of interest, write a marketing plan for the organization, or write an op-ed news piece highlighting some aspect of the organization. Think big—there are lots of charitable and service organizations who could use the talents you're willing to give away in exchange for the experience.

Apprenticeship Find someone who is doing what you want to do and offer to help out. You might shadow the owner of a small business for a short time, assist a writer with background research for her next book, or serve as an assistant to a local politician. Your goal is to gain skills, perspective, knowledge, and contacts. When you find that per-

TOM, AGE 29, CHICAGO

When Tom decided to leave corporate America, he took some interesting routes out of the cubicle. "I had been successful in sales for a large financial institution, making some decent money. But when I started spending more time on my volunteer work with nonprofit groups than my 'real' job, I realized that this wasn't the place for me," explains Tom. His area of passionate interest is the plight of children's education, particularly improving education in the inner cities. "I knew I couldn't learn this in a classroom setting; I needed to get out there, experience what's going on with education in Chicago, where I live."

So Tom left his corporate gig and immediately got a part-time job in the menswear section at an upscale department store to take care of his mortgage. This dreamfunder worked well for him because it was a commission-based position, which stimulated his selling instinct, and the people contact made it a rather enjoyable way to fund his inner-city sabbatical.

Tom developed his own approach to an apprenticeship by interviewing every expert and exploring every source of information he could get hold of. "Every person I talked to sparked some new ideas; I was feeling energized and yet overwhelmed by the intensity of the problems out there." Tom also volunteered as a tutor at an inner-city after-school program, as well as "reading everything I could get my hands on."

Tom gave himself a year for this sabbatical process, and he has a few months yet to go. "I've got several ideas in my head as far as my next move once this learning phase is over," he says. "One idea is to start my own nonprofit organization that would serve as a sort of umbrella group to tie together and create communication lines between a lot of the existing groups out there and the tremendous work they are all doing. I would never have thought of starting an organization myself, but by giving myself this time to truly research and process, I think I've started looking at things more innovatively and creatively."

son, call or write and directly ask for an apprenticeship. Tell him why you chose him and what qualities attract you to him. People love to have their egos massaged, and by asking to be someone's apprentice, you're giving a full body rub. If you get a negative response, you'll probably get a polite and reasonable explanation. You can then move on to your next candidate.

Sabbaticals are hands-on experiences directly related to where you want to be. You're going to do this on your free time and receive no income for it, so hold out until you find one that will truly help you move toward your goal.

2. Experiential Travel

Experiential travel is a mindfeed that will stimulate and challenge your internal resources so you can learn and grow. It provides a place and a time where you can listen closely to your heart and soul and discover what they are telling you.

Experiential travel provides the time and environment to do whatever helps you facilitate your deep thinking, whether rambling in your journal, going for a long walk, or taking a nap in a shaded hammock. But this kind of travel is not the traditional "vacation." Although you may use your weekends or vacation time, experiential travel means plucking yourself from your comfortable day-to-day environment and placing yourself in a starkly different environment. This kind of travel involves going native, seeing the world on a shoestring budget, wearing a backpack—not from behind the tinted windows of an air-conditioned tour bus. Once you remove yourself from the Club Med mindset and sling a pack on your back to head off for a youth hostel, boarding house, or tent, you open yourself up to

HOLLY, AGE 25, DALLAS

"I was getting so down on my job in brand management that I'd have these daily fantasies of just quitting and traveling the world. But in reality, that just isn't possible. I don't have the financial resources to do that, plus I have obligations to my family here that I need to be around for. So instead, for the next six months, I've planned some form of 'mini-experience' every weekend. It may be taking the train across town and wandering a neighborhood I've never been to, or throwing my camping gear in the car and driving straight north for three hours to see what I'll find. It's a bit more challenging to creatively come up with travel experiences in your own area, but I started making lists of things in the area I had never seen and I got lots of ideas. This is sort of my first step in figuring out what my next career steps are. I know I need to get out of this cubicle, but I'm so stressed out and swamped during the week that I can't open my mind and really think. I'm hoping these weekend experiences will stimulate some new perspectives."

provocative experiences that significantly increase your perspective on yourself and your place in the world. Experiential travel is a reality check, a wake-up call, an opportunity to see the real world where you shed the "tourist" label and become a local by accepting and enjoying the variety of cultural and environmental differences on this small planet.

The library and the Internet are valuable tools in planning an experiential travel mindfeed. But beware of travel guidebooks because they are written for tourists and will distract you from your goal. Try networking. Ask around, talk to people, or send out a message in a chat room or electronic bulletin board—something like, "Looking for a nontourist vacation site to get to know myself and the locals; any ideas?" You might also specify if you want something cheap and if you want to travel abroad or stay in the States.

Experiential travel should challenge you and open your eyes. It should fill your heart and soul with drive and determination. It should make you more determined than ever to leave the status quo behind.

There are a growing number of travel-related web sites. Most states and countries have an official web site that provides substantial, up-to-the-minute, practical information and links. Other interesting travel web sites include:

- **Hosteling International** (http://www.hostels.com)
- **Fodors** (http://www.fodors.com)
- **Lonely Planet** (http://www.lonelyplanet.com)

These sites offer continually updated travel resources, including specific information by country.

You might also try **Mungo Park** (http://www.mungopark.com). This is the on-line interactive adventure and environmental travel magazine by Microsoft. The editor, Richard Bangs, is the founder of Sobek Expeditions.

3. The Traditional Classroom

A mindfeed focusing on classroom learning may not be as creative and freewheeling as the other types, but for some people a traditional track is the best choice. Call it the "making a change but not taking the full plunge" option. Some of the other mindfeeds might seem a bit too risky, adventurous, or even complicated for some. A move back into the classroom will serve to move you from your current job situation into a totally different, more engaging environment. Graduate school, nondegree courses, continuing ed classes, or community school night classes all can provide features of a mindfeed you need.

Structure Classroom learning forces you to focus, learn, and grow. You have a schedule to follow and a curriculum all mapped out for you. In the very least, you know you'll learn *something*. On the downside, there may be academic bureaucracy and red tape to deal with, which probably won't feel much different than life on the corporate side, but just keep your goal in mind and don't sweat the small stuff.

Safety Going back to school is an acceptable part of leaving the corporate world. Mom, Dad, and friends won't bug you so much about wasting your life. Higher education has the aura of intelligence and attaches to you labels like *smart, bright, organized,* and *successful.* But be careful and stay focused; safety has its pitfalls. The academic world will try to steer you according to its own agenda. If you choose grad school, for instance, you'll be graduating with friends who will be doing the interview thing, whipping out résumés and crisply dry-cleaned suits. This is the place you're trying to get away from. Don't let a few years in the classroom cause you to lose touch and forget your LOCT lifestyle goals. Be prepared to give yourself a jump start at the end of your formal schooling. Keep yourself focused on your self-employment goals.

Links to Resources Academic connections open doors; individuals and organizations are more willing to share information and time with a student. You will also have use of the school's resources, which may include free use of electronic databases, Internet connections, library facilities, and career resource centers.

Time to Explore Although the whole LOCT thing is appealing, you may not be totally, 100 percent, positively sure what you want to do, and you don't feel comfortable making any major moves just yet. Your ideas are half-baked

According to a poll conducted by business schools themselves, the top entrepreneurship programs were at:

1) Babson College, Graduate School of Business
2) Wharton School of Business
3) University of California at Los Angeles (UCLA)
4) Harvard Business School

Tied for fifth place:

5) DePaul University
5) University of Southern California

Success, 9/95

ANNIE, AGE 28, SAN DIEGO

Grad school was the kind of mindfeed that Annie needed. "I wasn't ready to make the jump from A to Z while kissing off corporate America without going through all the other letters of the alphabet first," she says with a smile. "I think I may be typical of a lot of people my age out there thinking about leaving the corporate scene. I'm not a natural risk taker, and I need more time to think through and flesh out my ideas and what's next for me."

Annie worked in the financial industry for six years since college. Last fall she started working toward her master's in managerial communications—"an MBA without all the numbers," she explains. "School is shaking me up a bit, which is exactly what I need now. I need to expose myself to different ideas and different people, people who are out of the corporate-clone mindset that I am with every day at work." The people she's been meeting in class have been particularly stimulating to Annie. "The people I meet in class are just about all, in different ways, thinking about striking out on their own. It's good for me to expose myself to other people who are open to and looking for change. I think being around such inspirational stimulus will make it difficult for me to stay in my same corporate position once I'm done with school."

Being around similar people searching for their LOCT has inspired Annie and her classmates to creatively develop their own support structure. "I just e-mailed people in my class about the idea of starting sort of an entrepreneurial support group—an informal group that would meet regularly in which we would share our ideas and give each other feedback and encouragement." Annie is starting to brainstorm LOCT directions for herself. "I see myself doing relatively similar things to what I've been doing at my corporate job, giving training seminars and public speaking, but doing it on my own. I'm in contact with a couple of small, independent consulting firms that do this sort of work that I think I'd be able to do freelance work for to start developing a client base."

ALLYSON, AGE 30, LOS ANGELES

"I've had this idea in the back of my mind for a couple of years now: to open a coffeehouse that would be family-oriented, a kid-friendly sort of place. Serve coffee for adults and juice and stuff for kids. It would be the kind of place families could hang out at, play games, and just spend some quality time together. This idea never got anywhere because I was always so busy at the law firm where I work, and my travel schedule was out of control. I'd fantasize about the place, but that's as far as it went until I realized that I needed a bit more of a structured environment for me to get anywhere with this concept. So I signed up for a four-week course this summer at my local community college on how to write a business plan. The class meets on Saturday afternoons, so I won't have to miss it because of a work crisis, and I'll be creating the actual business plan as part of the class, so I'll have something concrete to start on. I think this classroom environment, plus being around other entrepreneurial people, is the push I need to move from talking about something to doing it."

and not quite there yet. Taking formal classes not only buys you time to cook your ideas, it provides the resources and connections to gather and organize the ingredients you may need. It's a holding tank of sorts, a temporary storage place that can be used to your advantage.

A jump start Many colleges, universities, and adult schools are recognizing the entrepreneurial spurt among our generation and are adapting their programs to meet these needs. If you can find the right program, you'll get more than a diploma at the end—you'll get the entrepreneurial tools you need to formalize your business plan.

Warning

On paper, mindfeeds create a rather romantic illusion. But whenever you put yourself in a situation where you are fully responsible for your own outcome with no deadlines, set guidelines, or criteria, you can easily end up stuck in the muddle. There's no set beginning and end, no established criteria for you to go by. So it's easy to shoot off in random directions, losing sight of your end goal and feeling no sense of accomplishment or achievement as you go along. With that in mind, here are some guidelines and ideas for planning your mindfeed.

Mindfeed Guidelines

Set Goals and Curriculum Setting goals may sound like a pretty basic, mundane concept, but when you're writing your own curriculum, it's important to define the educational road you'll be traveling. Then you'll have a definite beginning and end, which will determine your direction and define the elements and topics to include in your "coursework."

Start at the End What is your desired final result? What knowledge or understanding do you seek? As you begin to answer these questions, list the reasons why you want and need this new knowledge or experience. Are you aiming for: (1) a new skill, (2) information, or (3) experience? Your sabbatical quest will probably touch on all of these goals, but take some time to weed out what will be most beneficial to you in the end and then go after it. This will be far different from scanning a course catalog and choosing something because a three-sentence description sounds interesting. Now you're identifying and seeking out real-life situations that will fill in your educational gaps.

Take Your Time Finding just the right mindfeed isn't always easy, so take your time to explore the possibilities before you sign up. Your local public library is a good place to start some old-fashioned exploratory research. Check out books and magazine and newspaper articles. Take a close look at the bibliographies and sources cited in these resources. Use encyclopedias of associations, and don't forget to ask the librarian—he or she may know exactly where to find what you're looking for. And use the Internet for leads also; plugging in a key word that describes your field of interest into a search engine like Yahoo or Lycos will give you an overdose of information. This is a treasure hunt—you may be surprised where the search leads you.

KEEPING IT ALL TOGETHER

The ongoing theme in this preparing for self-employment stage is this: Keep focused. Know what your goals are and keep working on your plan for getting there. The biggest obstacle in this time of preparation is falling into limbo, shooting off in different directions, and not really learning

> "It's surprising how many people go through life without ever recognizing that their feelings toward other people are largely determined by their feelings toward themselves. If you're not comfortable within yourself, you can't be comfortable with others."
>
> —Sydney J. Harris

anything. That's why it's key to set up evaluation points to make sure things are on track and where you want them to be. It's sort of like a 15-point oil change; check your gears and make sure everything is running efficiently.

First, set a time frame to work from. It's arbitrary and might change, but give yourself some perspective to start from. At this point, how long do you predict it will take to reach your goal? Two months? Six months? A year? Whatever, fine. Write that date down.

Now, consider money. How much cash will these efforts cost? Maybe, ideally, nothing. One less thing to deal with. If not, what is your budget? What can you afford? If you need more money, how are you going to get it? Write down your budget. Don't forget to factor in the basics like transportation and phone costs too. Aim to financially manage yourself like you would any mini-business. Set halfway, quarterly, weekly (whatever works for you) points to give yourself a checkup. Are you where you need and expect to be? Did you get off track? What will you do better or differently in the future? What enhancements and improvements should you make?

The goal of these evaluations is to avoid falling into preparatory oblivion. No one else is steering your ship now—you are free to control and direct your life. With that freedom comes the onus of managing yourself effectively, keeping yourself moving and focused. The key is to get out of a one-track, one-way, one-job description mindset. While you're preparing your kiss-off journey, let yourself think creatively and expansively.

4

Self-Employment: The Meat and Potatoes

"Flying solo"

A friend of mine decided she was going to commit herself to an adult rite of passage: She was going to cook Thanksgiving dinner by herself. Her parents and boyfriend would have Thanksgiving dinner at her place. They were going to eat from real plates; she was pulling out all the stops. She read up on Martha Stewartesque variations on the traditional favorites, overshopped for multiple gourmet ingredients, called her mother for the family's favorite recipes, and ran back to the store for "those cute little mini-gourd things to decorate the table with." She decided the stuffing recipe printed on the back of the crouton bag might be easier after all and called Mom again.

What was the problem? She was getting caught up in the details of her project and was losing sight of the big, important picture: Put the damn turkey in the oven. Focus on the big-picture, essential tasks and the smaller, less critical particulars will fall in place and work themselves out. Act on one thing rather than stress about everything.

So it goes with many of us would-be LOCTs as we start to take action on starting our self-employed life: We get so overwhelmed by all the details that we lose sight of the big picture. Like my Thanksgiving friend, you need to simply start cooking that bird.

Understand that it's really hard to utterly ruin a turkey. It might come out dry or unevenly cooked, but rarely is a Thanksgiving bird so inedible that the family feast is relegated to take-out from Boston Market. It's the same with setting up your self-employed life. You're going to make some mistakes. You'll look back and recognize things you would do differently if you were starting over. But if you get the basics down, it's hard to screw up.

SIMPLICITY PLANNING 101

Keep it simple. The transition from a corporate situation, where probably all administrative matters from accounting to ordering paper clips were taken care of by someone else, to self-employment, where you're responsible for everything, can be daunting. Here's the trick: Keep it simple. Focus on two things:

"I see other people my age as much more driven than our parents and grandparents. Our parents got their nice little job (which they stayed with until retirement) and their nice little house, and that was considered the 'good life.' People my age tend to look at that and say, 'So what? What's the big deal?' We see the nice little house and nice little job as 'starting out' rather than 'the good life.' I look around and see a number of late twentysomethings and early thirtysomethings who have accomplished amazing things already."

—Posted on the "Sandwich Generation" folder on America OnLine

- Identify what has to be done and do it as simply and economically as possible.
- Utilize the support system that's already in place to your advantage.

This may be reminiscent of the corporate world, but the reality is we have to work within other bureaucratic systems: the government, insurance companies, banks, the boys with blue suits, and others. There are rules, regulations, and protocol that must be followed, forms to fill out, and dues to pay. So don't make it any more complicated than it has to be. Don't do, worry about, or pay more than you have to and learn to utilize the system to your advantage.

Don't feel that you need to know everything on everything. You don't. You can't. You'll develop migraines trying. There will always be legal, accounting, insurance, and other issues coming up. The key is to be "educated enough." Keep yourself informed as best you can. Read reference material. Ask questions. Get different opinions. Invest in paid professional counsel when needed. Don't stress.

THE SELF-EMPLOYMENT NONBUSINESS PLAN

Warning: The following is a twist on the traditional notion of business start-up planning. We aren't building a lifestyle around a single business idea. Rather, we are building multiple business ideas around the lifestyle we want. Your business plan is a working, personal document created to organize your individual self-employment, LOCT philosophy. Your plan never has to be put in a blue vinyl Kinko's binder and mass distributed for review and critique. It is for your use only.

Think of this type of plan as a cross between a self-reflection journal and a Filofax, a tool for both reflection and planning, for your eyes only. With that in mind, take a notebook and pen and mark off five to ten pages for each of these categories:

- Purpose statement
- Description of product/services
- Marketing
- Management status
- Timetable
- Finances

"This sure sounds like a typical business plan," you say. Hang on, friend. Like I said, it's a twist on the traditional business-plan concept. The format is typical but the content is not. So keep that notebook handy and write down some initial thoughts and impressions for each of these sections as explained below. Date your entries. You'll be using this notebook as a tool, an ongoing resource of your LOCT growth. And one other thing to remember: You're the only one seeing this. Every sentence doesn't need to be complete and perfect, or every concept realistic and well thought-out. The key is to write down something, anything, stream of consciousness, whatever. Just get started.

Purpose Statement

The reasons you are or want to soon be self-employed. Don't panic. Just jot down some preliminary thoughts. What is your reasoning and philosophy for wanting a LOCT life? What are your expectations? Some examples:

- Want control of my time. Need flexibility, the ability to do things according to my own schedule.
- Think I'd be good at being my own boss. That would challenge me more than just about anything in the corporate scene.
- Need to be able to pursue various things. Need variety and lots of projects on my plate. That's when I'm most creative.
- Want to create a balance between my work and free time so I will have more opportunities to build the relationships in my life.

Description of Product/Services

What are your "sellable" and "marketable" qualities and talents? Think of your self-employed, LOCT self as a product. What are your key strengths? Think beyond traditional résumé lingo and brainstorm other criteria that make you unique. Examples:

- Power researcher. Good at utilizing creative means to gather information.
- Can schmooze anything and anyone very well over the phone.
- Able to help people adjust to group situations quickly. Have the knack for making people feel comfortable in new situations.

Marketing

What ways and opportunities do you have to sell yourself and your abilities? What contacts and resources do you have to get started? Examples:

- Strong relationships with all past employers. Opportunity for possible part-time work.
- Have wide range of local contacts to start networking with.
- Understand how to use the Internet effectively and as a resource for building business.

Management Status

How is the "boss" (i.e., you) doing? What are your strengths right now? What are some things you'd like to work on and improve? Examples:

- Very motivated and committed. Ideas have been festering for so long that I'm ready to roll.
- Need to give overall health a boost. Cubicle life has taken its toll. Need to start exercising regularly and eating healthier.
- Need to work toward keeping all aspects of life in balance. Start taking the time to pursue other hobby interests.

Timetable

What is your time frame? What is on your calendar? What other events/opportunities are coming up? Examples:

- Will be fully vested in profit sharing at corporate job in six months. After that will be the ideal time to leave.
- Apartment lease is up this spring. Now is a good time to start brainstorming places to relocate. Maybe plan an exploratory trip? Perhaps there is some info on the Internet?

- I'm turning thirty in two years. I not only want to make this self-employed transition happen but I want to own a condo by then too.

Finances

Where are you financially? What do you need to start your business and maintain your living expenses? What are some creative alternatives to achieving these things? Examples:

- Need a computer setup quickly. Check into sharing the cost with a buddy who is aiming to do something similar.
- My first step will be to track my spending this month. Then I'll know where I stand and where I can start cutting back.
- What would my condo rent for if I rented it out and traveled for a year?

LEGAL ISSUES

The following legal, financial, and insurance matters really won't have much to do with how your business is perceived from the outside or how you interact with future clients and customers. But they're important operational issues that you need to consider in order to make informed decisions so you can utilize the system to your advantage. The following is some general information to get you started.

Step One: Decide on Structure

All the businesses in the country, from Ted Turner's enterprises to the neighborhood lemonade stand, technically fall into one of three categories: Sole proprietorship, partnership, or corporation.

Option One: Sole Proprietor A sole proprietorship is a business owned and operated by one person. From a legal perspective, you and the business are one and the same. The business is a legal extension of yourself, so whatever happens to the business, good or bad, happens to you. Profit, loss, lawsuits, financial trouble, whatever, you are totally responsible.

Pros Sole proprietorships are relatively simple. They are typically easy to start and maintain. They involve little red tape, minimal forms to fill out, and fewer government regulations and fees. They usually cost practically nothing to start, no legal or accounting fees needed, maybe a nominal filing fee with your local or state government. Many small businesses begin this way, and it may be the most appealing option for those of you just starting out as a LOCT. By setting yourself up as a sole proprietorship, you are a legitimate, operating business, and you can start taking advantage of tax deductions. Sole proprietorship profits and losses are tied to your personal finances and are reported on your personal tax return by filing an IRS Schedule C/Form 1040. This can be beneficial (i.e., you pay less). For example, if you're launching your business while still on the corporate scene, any loss from that business can be deducted from your regular job earnings, reducing your taxes. From a tax perspective, it can be to your benefit to experiment and make mistakes while still on the company payroll. From the same perspective, there are advantages to following the "layering" approach to self-employment by having multiple businesses in operation (each requires a separate Schedule C, which is no big deal): A loss from one business can offset profits from another business, lowering your tax debt.

Cons In a sole proprietorship, you and your business are one. That means if the business goes up in smoke, so do you. No business is immune from liability, and some have greater potential for it. You can always move from a sole proprietorship to a corporation down the line, perhaps when you have more at stake to lose, such as a home.

How to Get Started Plan on making a round of phone calls and being transferred from one person to another before you get all the information you need. Start by calling both your county government and your city/local government. Your county government will know of any paperwork you will need to complete for your state. Your city/local government will know if there are any additional restrictions, licensing, or forms to complete on a local level. The specific department you call may vary in name from state to state and city to city. As a first step, open the phone book and check under:

- the "blue pages" that list various governmental departments
- "Government" in the yellow pages
- your specific county or city name in the white pages

Sometimes the department you need to start with will be clearly identified as "business licensing." But, given governmental bureaucracy, it probably won't be so clear. If there isn't a general information number, try the

department of revenue/treasurer, someone there should be able to answer your questions or direct your calls. Simply ask, "I am interested in starting a sole proprietorship in XYZ town that will be a (fill in the blank—describe your business). What paperwork do I need to complete?" Most of these forms should be fairly self-explanatory and have minimal (ten to fifty dollars) fees associated with them.

Option Two: Partnership A partnership is an association of two or more individuals who jointly own the business. From a legal perspective, partnerships are viewed as sole pro-

Remember, the government wants to help and encourage you to start and grow your business. This may not always seem like the case, especially when you are trying to find out the concrete steps you need to take to start a business and are bounced around to a slew of department receptionists. Many cities and geographic regions will publish a comprehensive "getting your business started" information packet, clearly organizing and outlining all the necessary legal steps you need to take to get your idea up and running. The trick is identifying which department has this information. Try calling a nongovernmental agency, the Chamber of Commerce, as a first step. It's the chamber's mission to help local businesses start and grow, and you'll find them surprisingly helpful in pointing you in the right direction. Look under "Chamber of Commerce" in the white pages of the phone book.

prietorships that are divided among several people. All partners share the good stuff and the bad: profits, loss, legal responsibility, and so on.

Partnerships are bound by a set of agreements drawn up when the business is formed, detailing how the business is divided up, usually based on the amount of money each partner contributes. The partnership itself pays no taxes, but it files a tax form with the government (Form 1065) detailing the partnership's income and expense and each partner's share of the income or loss. Each partner then reports his or her share of income on their regular Form 1040 using a Schedule E. Each partner thereby pays taxes on his or her portion individually; the partnership itself doesn't pay any taxes with its return. As with sole proprietorships, the business is inseparable from the partners. Partners share the rewards and the risks.

Pros Partnerships can multiply strengths and balance out weaknesses. There's also a greater sense of responsibility to the business; you're in this together. Additionally, there are financial benefits to partnerships as two people are now bringing start-up money to the business versus just one individual.

Cons Enter partnerships with caution. For better or worse, you're liable and responsible for all decisions made by the partnership. Further discussion about various LOCT relationships is ahead in chapter 7, but don't jump into a partnership without a lot of forethought. Partnerships can be very appealing, as you're no longer kissing off corporate America alone. There's safety in numbers. But ask yourself honestly: Is this something I could do on my own? Am I simply using a partner as a crutch, or is there truly a significant benefit here? Can my partner (or partners) and I handle conflict and disagreement amiably?

If you do choose a partnership, approach it as a pragmatic, objective business deal. Don't let the blissful cloud of friendship overshadow the facts. The more detail that can be outlined ahead of time, the more up-front discussions of management practices and philosophy, the greater the chances of success. Remember, too, that all partnerships will most likely end eventually. Someone will be ready to move on, try something new, at differing speeds than the other partners. Expect this situation; talk about it and how you will handle it beforehand.

Limited Partnerships Limited, or "silent," partnerships involve partners who contribute money and usually nothing else. They typically don't have a say in the day-to-day operations or management, and no liability risk beyond their invested money. All authority and decisions are the responsibility of the full partners. When would you use a limited partnership? Typically, when you need extra cash that you can't get through bank loans. You approach an outside investor or family member who contributes money.

Getting Started Partnerships and limited partnerships are closely regulated by the government and involve trickier legal issues. All involved should seek professional legal and accounting assistance. Start by contacting the same organizations outlined above for sole proprietorships; ask what different/additional paperwork is necessary for a partnership. Get as far as you can, gather as much information as possible, before consulting a professional. Aside from governmental forms, you will want to take things one step further and have your own partnership agreements in writing, outlining the exact ownership structure, how decisions/operations will be handled, how a future buyout/breakup will occur, and so forth. There are standard partnership agreement forms that you can pick up at a stationery or office supply store; however, depending on the complexity of your business and the amount of financials involved, you may still want to consult a professional. For the basics, none of this should be too complicated or costly, but it will still probably cost in the hundreds of dollars.

Option Three: Corporations A corporation is a business established as a distinct legal entity. It is completely separate from the person or people who own it. What does this mean? In a way, you're literally creating a "being." This "being," the corporation, can do just about everything you can—it can make or lose money, purchase property, pay taxes, and so on.

Before we get into pros and cons, it's important to differentiate between the two different types of corporations: standard/C and subchapter S. A standard/C corporation gives owners liability protection; taxes are paid at a higher corporate rate by the business itself. A subchapter S corporation is sort of a combination of sole proprietorship and full corporation. It provides the same liability protection, but taxes are paid at a personal rate. Subchapter S corporations provide the liability benefits of a corporation without complicated tax turmoil.

Pros One of the primary benefits of incorporating is to keep your personal assets legally separate from the business. If You, Inc. goes under, you won't necessarily lose your house, sports car, Jacuzzi—any assets that the business doesn't technically "own."

Cons As if life wasn't complicated enough, incorporating adds to the confusion. There are more legal and accounting fees, not just for start-up, but on a continual basis as you will have more reporting accountability to the government. There is much more time and money involved.

Getting Started The decision of whether or not to incorporate is a complicated one. Most LOCTs, myself included, can start off just fine as sole proprietors. We don't have that much in assets, so we don't have that much to lose. Consequently, the complication of incorporation is probably unnecessary for most self-employed businesses to get started. Don't let this corporate quandary slow you down. Get out there quickly as a sole proprietor, and when the time, need, and money warrant, find a good accountant and/or lawyer to lead you through some solid incorporation options. However, as discussed with partnerships, do your up-front research on your own and save on professional fees. Each state has its own paperwork and regulations regarding corporations. Start by contacting your state governmental offices; most states will have a specific department entitled "corporations." Call them first for general information and the necessary paperwork to start a corporation.

Step Two: Other Fun Stuff

And the legal games continue. When you become self-employed, you're stepping into a big pit of rules and regulations, permits, fees, forms, and more forms. But don't despair. Apply the "educated enough" theory; deal with things as you need to. Continue to be proactive, do your research, ask questions, and seek answers. The following issues may not apply at all, but they are key ones to be aware of.

Filing a "DBA" ("Doing Business As") If you are doing business under a fictitious name, you will need to fill out a DBA form ("Doing Business As"). These forms are usually handled through your county office. Try calling the county clerk office first, as this is the department that typically handles the processing.

A fictitious name may sound a little fishy, but all it means is you are doing business under a name other than your own. So, therefore, most businesses have DBAs. What this form does is officially state to the public that you are the person behind this company's name. The form isn't complicated, and the filing fee will probably range between twenty and a hundred dollars, depending on where you live. Some places, like Chicago, require that you take out a small ad in the newspaper, "stating for the record to the public" that you are operating under this business name. You will need a copy of your completed DBA certificate to open up a business bank account that can accept checks made out to the business name and to obtain an EIN (Employee Identification Number). DBA filings do not apply to corporations in most states unless the corporation is doing business under a name other than its own. The incorporation paperwork includes the same name registration process as a DBA filing does for sole proprietorships and partnerships.

Filing an "EIN" ("Employee Identification Number")

No surprise: When you start a business, the government wants to know where you are and how to track your income. There are two ways the government identifies you: your social security number or an Employee Identification Number (EIN). The EIN is used to track employee paperwork, whether you hire employees or use independent contractors. If you are a sole proprietor with no employees, you probably don't need an EIN. However, you can get an EIN without employees. Why? Some government forms, like tax resale certificates (see next section), require them.

To get an EIN, you need to file IRS form SS-4. One point of advice if you do not have employees: Write in big letters on this form, "For Identification Purposes Only." Otherwise, the IRS will assume you have employees and will start automatically sending you piles of paperwork you don't need.

Seller's Permits If you're going to be selling tangible items, your state and local government are going to want you to collect applicable sales tax and forward it to them. It is your responsibility to collect and submit state sales tax, usually once a year. These "seller's permit" forms can be a bit complicated to file because different counties within states often charge different rates. This can get especially confusing if you are doing some mail-order business because many states require that you calculate the sales tax rate based on where the item was delivered.

Another sales tax–related issue is resale. Sales tax is paid only once, by the customer eventually buying the product

Are you starting to feel overwhelmed by all these IRS forms you need to find and file? Don't panic. Despite the IRS having an evil image of audits and red tape, as an organization they truly do want you, the small business owner, to succeed. With that in mind, start things on a clean slate and take advantage of the number of resources the IRS provides. There are three key ways to get forms and information:

- Stop by your local IRS office, usually listed as a department in the blue governmental pages of the phone book or under United States Government in the white pages. Post offices and libraries will also have a large selection of tax forms and informational publications around tax time.
- Check out the IRS web site (http://www.irs.ustreas.gov). Given the bureaucracy of the organization, the IRS web site is quite useful and is continually being updated and enhanced.
- Call the IRS directly at (800) 829-1040. If you want to speak to a person, call during normal business hours; however, forms and publications are available twenty-four hours a day via a fax-on-demand system. You can also obtain information via this 800 number on downloading forms and information from the Internet. Try to get your questions answered before the April 15 panic, when phone lines and IRS staff are swamped.

for use. The responsibility for collecting this tax lies with the person or company who is conducting the final sale with the consumer. What this means is if your business sells wholesale goods to retail outlets, it is that store's responsibility to collect and submit sales tax to the state, not yours. However, if you are buying raw materials that you are going to use to create finished products, you don't need to pay sales tax when you buy the materials.

For example, if you're making jewelry, the raw material you use to make the actual product, such as the beads, is sales tax–exempt when you buy it from a supplier. (It's called "buying wholesale.") The beads are exempt because you are using them for resale. When you sell your work to consumers, you are responsible for collecting the sales tax. If you sell to a boutique, however, then that store is responsible for collecting the tax. However, if you buy some tools for making the jewelry, these are not tax exempt because you are not reselling the tools.

Where do you get these seller's permits? The state agencies issuing seller's permits (sometimes called resale certificates) vary from state to state. Generally it may fall under the State Sales Tax Commission. Once you contact the appropriate state agency, someone there can advise you if there are any additional city/local taxes you need to be aware of. Service businesses in most states are not subject to sales tax, but check with your state taxation office for specifics.

Regulation Overload As you can see, small businesses are faced with seemingly endless regulation hurdles. It can be daunting; you've never had to deal with so many small details before. You may feel that there's no one to help you, and that every agency gives you the runaround.

Make it easier on yourself by calling some organizations who are genuinely interested in attracting and helping new businesses. The national office of the Small Business Administration (SBA) at (800) 827-5722 can refer you to some local business groups in your area, such as the Service Corps of Retired Executives (SCORE). SCORE is a nonprofit group of retired business executive volunteers who want to help new, young businesses succeed.

Feeling on info-overload with all of this business start-up stuff? Turn to the Internet; there are a growing number of on-line resources for the budding entrepreneur. Here are just a few to get started:

Zinc: For Young Entrepreneurs

(http://www.inc.com)

Sponsored by *Inc. Magazine*, Zinc is an on-line feature that focuses specifically on issues important to our generation. There are a range of interviews and profile pieces of the struggles various young entrepreneurs are facing. Check out the Inc. homepage for other business start-up resources.

Entrepreneurial Edge Online

(http://www.edgeonline.com)

Published by the Edward Lowe Foundation, this web site is an on-line extension of *Entrepreneurial Edge* magazine. Check out the "Interactive Toolbox" section, which contains training modules that teach a range of business skills, from accounting to sales.

The Center for Entrepreneurial Leadership

(http://www.entreworld.org)

Sponsored by the Kauffman Foundation, Entreworld is a nonprofit, web-based resource to stimulate and support entrepreneurship. Also contains information on entrepreneurship within the nonprofit sector.

ACCOUNTING ISSUES

Step One: Deduct!

"Deduction, deduction, What's your function?" A Schoolhouse Rock reference for the accounting scene. The same philosophy applied to legal issues earlier in the chapter applies to accounting as well: Learn the system so it works for you. And no whining please! No groans of, "But I'm not an accountant, I can't do this stuff." Apply that simplicity theory again. Realize you're not aiming for perfection; you don't need to learn everything under the financial sun. Remember, accounting is far from rocket science. You're not the first to go through this.

First, to be successfully self-employed you need a fundamental attitude shift toward spending money. You need to look at every aspect of your life as potentially business related, and potentially deductible. Now of course, not everything is. But a lot of things will be, or can be, if you make the conscious effort and constantly think along these lines. Keep those receipts; stay organized and on top of things. It's money back in your pocket.

According to the IRS, you can deduct expenses from your gross income if they are an "ordinary and necessary" part of your work. Now what is "ordinary" to one person may not be to another. Use your judgment; pull in an accountant's advice when necessary. The deductions and numbers (i.e., maximums/minimums, percentages) involved are in a continual state of flux; the IRS will always have the latest information.

The following are some deductions that are typical and yet often overlooked or not taken full advantage of by self-employed people: (Please note that these deductions change; check with your local IRS office for current information.)

Automobile If you own a car, pick up a mileage log and start tracking your miles. They are small, user-friendly books you can pick up at any office supply store. Keep it in your car, and any time you take a trip or run an errand that

A helpful starter kit to get from the IRS is their "Business Tax Kit." Call (800) TAX-FORM (800-829-3676) to order the kit, which contains an assortment of IRS forms and publications to get you started, including:

Forms:

- SS-4, Application for Employer Identification Number (EIN)
- 1040-ES, Estimated Tax for Individual Publications
- 334, Tax Guide for Small Businesses
- 583, Starting a Business and Keeping Records
- 910, Guide for Free Tax Services

includes something business-related, enter the date, mileage, and a description into the book. Picking up office supplies, going to the post office, or going to a social event where you know you'll be networking are all business-related expenses. Don't forget any tolls and parking fees. You then tally up the mileage at the end of the year, multiply it by the going rate per mile (for the 1997 tax year, the IRS allows a deduction of $.315 per mile), and that total is deducted. It may take a while to get in the habit of writing down all your mileage, but those miles add up. (The mileage log is the best documentation for the IRS. Photocopy the log periodically as backup.) I bought a used car for $3000 three years ago, and I've recouped the money spent on the car through tracking my miles and taking this deduction.

Bank Charges We'll cover setting up a separate account later in this section. But from a deduction perspective, if there are any fees or service charges associated with this account, those are deductions.

Books and Publications The purchase of any book, magazine, or journal that is related to your business is deductible.

Business Gifts An overlooked deduction, especially at holiday time. You can deduct gifts to business associates, up to a maximum of twenty-five dollars per person, per year.

Dues You can deduct dues to any related professional association.

Education You can write off any classes, conferences, seminars, and other educational costs to improve or maintain skills related to the business. The key phrase here is *improve or maintain*. You can't deduct for educational expenses not related to your business. Still, this can be a nice incentive to continue your "lifetime learning" quest and write it off.

Entertainment You can deduct business meals with clients, advisors, associates—any entertainment related to your business and during which business was discussed or conducted. Entertaining in your own home qualifies as well. Remember to keep track of receipts and be sure to record who was there and what business was conducted (we'll discuss easy ways to keep records via the computer in the next section). The IRS particularly scrutinizes these deductions, as they have been abused in the past. You can only deduct a percentage of entertainment expenses (currently 50 percent, but subject to change), so there's no free lunch.

Equipment Computers and other equipment are usually deductible by one of two ways—either through depreciation (by writing off a percentage every year) or a one-time write-off (the current maximum is $13,500, but subject to change). Your total deduction cannot be more than the total amount of money you make.

Insurance All business-related insurance is deductible. You currently can deduct 40 percent of your health-insurance premiums.

Interest Any interest payments on business debts are deductible.

Office Furniture Anything used for business purposes only, in your home office, is deductible—desks, chairs, bookcases, file cabinets, and so on.

On-line Services Fees are deductible if used for business.

Postage/Shipping Stamps, rental on P.O. boxes, mailing permits, and so on are all deductible if used for business, likewise for FedEx and UPS charges.

Printing/Photocopying Save those Kinko's receipts; all photocopies are a deductible expense. Save even those small receipts for just a couple of copies; collectively these will add up.

Professional Fees Fees paid to lawyers, accountants, designers, and so forth are all deductible.

Repairs The bright side of equipment breakdown is that you can write it off.

Supplies Consumable supplies, down to each and every paper clip, are deductible.

Telephone If you have one phone line in your home, you can deduct long-distance business-related charges only. But you'll need two lines anyway, for faxing and on-line convenience, so it will probably be more of a savings to install a second line, do all of your business calling on that line, and write off all charges for the line.

Travel Business-related travel costs are deductible, including public transportation and cab fares. You can't deduct "commuting" costs, but as a self-employed person you probably won't have any.

Home Sweet Office Deduction Do take the home office deduction if you can, but do so with caution. Yes, it is a valid, profitable deduction to take. Just make sure your documentation is in order and you understand every aspect. To take the home office deduction, you must meet two strict criteria (and remember the IRS loves to audit those who take the home office deduction):

- The area you claim for your office must be an exclusive and regular place for business; that is, it is used for business and nothing else.
- It must be your principal place for business, that is, you do the majority of your business from there.

Don't avoid taking this deduction; it's perfectly legitimate and I've been taking it for years. Just make sure you have all your ducks in a row and keep impeccable records.

To claim this deduction, you'll need to complete IRS Form 8829. The form includes a formula for figuring the percentage of your living space dedicated to your office. You can then deduct that magic percentage from your rent, utilities (electric, gas), and so on. For homeowners, this means a prorated portion of your mortgage interest and depreciation on your house. This deduction can also include any fix-up costs to get your home office ready, such as painting or decorating costs (wallpaper, carpets, lamps, furniture). A couple of key points to remember:

- Take photos of your office "at work" from all angles for documentation.
- If you live in a studio, you won't meet the "exclusive place for business" criteria since you do other things in that room as well, so consider moving to a one-bedroom place. If you think you can't afford it, think again; do the numbers. Make the bedroom your sole office, put the bed (or better yet, pull-out couch) in the living room, and make that your bedroom. I did this for a couple of years, and the home office deduction more than recouped the extra rent. I had more space overall and a decent office.

Step Two: Separate Financial Records

Make things easier on yourself and open a separate checking account to track all your business expenses. If you're operating as a sole proprietor and all income checks are made out to you, you should set up another personal account at the bank where you currently have an account. If you need to be able to accept and write checks under your business name, you need to open up a business checking account. You will need to bring in your DBA form to the bank to establish that account. Shop around for a good deal on a business checking account, especially if you don't think you will be having a lot of transactions and check processing immediately. The bank fees often associated with business checking can add up.

Also, it's a good idea to obtain a separate credit card to use solely for business. Number one, record keeping will be a lot simpler. Number two, by having separate accounts for "business" and "personal" money, the IRS will view your records as "clean" and your business as legit.

Step Three: Keep Good Records and Use the Computer

If you're experiencing information overload by now with all of these receipts and deductions to keep track of, relax. Call on our friend, the computer, for keeping track of everything.

There are a number of incredibly easy-to-use accounting software packages that make record keeping easier by leaps and bounds. I use Quicken, one of the leading financial packages that get you up and running in no time. Quicken and others like it will cost you about fifty to seventy-five dollars.

Of course you still must enter your numbers manually at the keyboard. But it's easier than you think, even for those of us whose idea of filing receipts is sticking them in the back of a drawer. Some pointers:

- Get into a keyboarding routine. Maybe on Sunday night, for example, you dump out your wallet and enter in receipts.
- Keep the receipts organized. The simplest, quickest thing to do is stick them in an envelope labeled by month. Don't put them all in one folder, mixed with other receipts and bills.
- Keep all your receipts, invoices, canceled checks, and so on for at least five years. Your actual tax returns should be kept indefinitely, especially as a self-employed person.

Step Four: Learn the Tax Game Before a Tax Crisis

Avoid the April panic. Start familiarizing yourself with the tax paperwork and systems as soon as you enter self-employment, not as panic sets in when taxes are due. Some key documents and details to get acquainted with:

- Schedule C. This is a sort of profit/loss statement for your business that shows the IRS how much money you made. You fill this out as part of the 1040 long form. Yes, you figured it out: No more 1040EZ forms. Get a copy of the Schedule C and become familiar with it. It isn't brain surgery, but it can be daunting if you first look at it on April 14.
- 1099s. These are like W2s for the self-employed. For example, if you did some work as an independent contractor, the person or company who hired you to do the work needs to report the amount of income you earned to the IRS. You then receive a 1099 confirming that amount.

Understand what kind of tax you're paying. In addition to income tax, solo entrepreneurs pay self-employment tax, a combination of Social Security and Medicare taxes. This is news to you? Yes, back in the corporate world, when you worked for someone else, your employer paid for half of this, but now you're paying all of this tax. If you're working solo part-time while still at a full-time job, your "regular" income will be reported on the 1040 form, and any business income will go on a Schedule C.

As a solo entrepreneur, because no taxes are withheld from your earnings, you are required to pay quarterly estimated taxes. However, when you start out you probably have no idea what your income will be, so this guesstimate is a shot in the dark. Don't panic. The penalties for paying all taxes in one lump sum in April are relatively small. Your first year it probably won't make much of a difference. Once you complete your first Schedule C, you will have a better idea of your tax burden. You are then responsible for paying 90 percent of your taxes by April 15, both state and federal.

The key here is to be careful your first couple of years. Since no deduction for taxes is taken from the money you make, your perception of your wealth may be skewed. You may think you have more money than you do, and with a starting business, you'll probably come up with lots of ways to use it. This is where computer accounting programs come in handy; just a few keystrokes and you'll know where your finances stand, what your income is to date, and what your taxes are like.

Make sure you are operating a legitimate "business" versus a "hobby." The IRS keeps close tabs on individuals who consistently run "businesses" at a loss just to cash in on the deductions. According to the IRS, a business must make a profit three years out of five; otherwise it is considered a "hobby." Keep this in mind as you enter year three.

HEALTH INSURANCE ISSUES

Yes, Virginia, there is health insurance for the self-employed. Not nearly as sexy as deductions and corporations, health insurance is something we'd all rather avoid. But we need to remember one of the core LOCT philosophies: Be self-sufficient, responsible for yourself. Think back to the discussion on "confident self-sufficiency" in chapters 1 and 2. We're responsible for ourselves now, sailing our own ship. Think of health insurance as investing in yourself. My early experience with health insurance was haphazard: I signed with the first company that came along, without a full understanding of the policy. I've been lucky so far in that I haven't had any disasters, but luck is hardly a safe bet. I knew I needed insurance, but I didn't know where to start.

With all the press about rising health costs and turmoil within the health insurance industry, it's no wonder we avoid dealing with this one. But there is probably no other insurance that can have as great an impact on you, the solo entrepreneur. No one plans on getting sick, but we need a plan to protect us if we do. The main purpose of health insurance is to prevent any major illness or accident from wiping you out financially. The following material will give you a look at a few of the ways to find health insurance.

Cash In on COBRA

If you are still employed by someone else who provides health insurance, check to see if you can continue your insurance through a COBRA extension after you've left the job. This entails continuing the same coverage you had on the job. Be prepared, however, as you will be paying higher premiums; now you're paying for the whole enchilada. Previously, your employer probably paid for part. Utilizing COBRA will give you an easy insurance option as you make the LOCT transition. COBRA may be expensive, but at least you'll be covered while you shop around for health insurance that fits your budget and your needs.

Find Your Own Plan

There are usually time limits on COBRA, and eventually you will need to find a policy of your own. Don't wait until the final seconds of COBRA run out before you start shopping around. Choose a policy and get your application approved before your existing policy runs out so you can smoothly transition from one plan to another.

Where do you start looking for a plan? Your best bet is first to ask other LOCTs. Where do they get their policies? Are they satisfied? Check out any policies that are offered through various groups and associations, such as professional or alumni organizations. When the insurance company is working with a larger group, rates tend to be lower.

Investigate any "major medical" type policies. Under these policies, you're basically covered for the long-term and/or costly medical expenses. You'll be paying out of pocket for checkups and office visits, but your premiums will usually be a lot lower. With this type of traditional plan, there is usually a yearly deductible to meet before the plan kicks in. Most traditional plans also work with a network of doctors; stay within the network and you're covered.

Investigate the policy before signing on. A glossy, professional-looking policy brochure can hide a lot of unscrupulous business practices. Try to go with a big company with a high insurance rating. Your local library will have books

LAURA, AGE 27, ATLANTA

Laura is a dabbler, a brainstormer of new business ideas. "I had worked as a teacher and at some nonprofit organizations, but I always knew that I was destined to be an entrepreneur. It was always just a question of when would the timing be right," she explains. Laura's life started evolving to "right place–right time" about two years ago. "That was when I was living in New York City and started experimenting with various small businesses. I started an errand delivery business, did some party planning, and investigated the concept of a national wedding registry linked by an 800 number." None of these ideas panned out. "It was a combination of wrong timing and simply that once I got into the concept, I didn't enjoy it very much. But I feel like I really learned a lot about myself and about running a business by experimenting like that. And they were small business endeavors, so I really didn't have to invest or lose much money." Laura was then ready to move on to her "big" business idea. "At first I really had no idea of what I wanted to do, so I read a lot and basically observed other businesses starting up. I first went to a paint-your-own-pottery shop in Philadelphia. Today there are a lot of these places across the country, stores where you can go and paint pottery and bisqueware, and the store will fire and glaze them for you. I quickly became addicted to that place. I never considered myself a very artistic person, but the stuff I created there came out looking really nice and usable."

She then started researching starting a paint-your-own-pottery shop in Atlanta. "I always loved Atlanta, ever since I went to school there," Laura explains. "Since I was starting a business from the ground up, I figured this was my opportunity to also move where I wanted to live." Laura researched and educated herself on the business in a number of creative, cost-effective ways:

- Took a business class at a local nonprofit center aimed at helping women entrepreneurs. "This class taught me a lot of the basic start-up issues, like accounting, and it also put me in touch with a lot of inspiring women who were in the same situation I was," says Laura.

- Worked at a coffeehouse. (One of her ideas to differentiate her place was to serve coffee drinks and snacks as well, so she wanted to gain an understanding of the business.)

- Took a business-plan writing class at a local college. "This was really helpful because it put me in touch with the university resources, so I could get lots of feedback and advice as I created and refined my business plan."

- Volunteered at an arts-and-crafts day camp. "I knew a big part of the pottery store's business would be kids and kids' birthday parties, so I wanted to observe and work with children as they did various crafts. I also had the idea, again to differentiate my store, to offer crafts other than just pottery—things like jewelry-making and tie-dying. I'm really not a 'crafty' person by nature, so volunteering at the camp gave me concrete ideas on how to do other types of crafts," explains Laura.

- Paid a consultant to teach her the paint-your-own-pottery business. "This was my major investment, but worth it. These pottery stores were already booming in NYC, and one of these store's owners was also a consultant for business start-ups like me. I gained his understanding of and experience in the business, learned from his mistakes, and saved myself a lot of time and money," says Laura. Her paint-your-own-pottery store, Art & Soul Art and Crafts Cafe, has been open for almost two years now. "Things are overall going well," says Laura. "I've learned that it takes time to get a business up and running. For the past two years, Art & Soul has been my waking passion." She's starting to think about ways to expand to other new, but related ideas, such as distributing specialized bisqueware to other pottery shops across the country and working as a consultant to other aspiring entrepreneurs who want to open similar shops in other cities.

ranking insurance companies. Bigger companies typically have deeper pockets. Call your state insurance regulation office to see if there are any complaints filed against the policy you are looking at. Ask your doctor or call the billing department of your local hospital and get their opinion on the policy you are considering.

Play the Uninsured Crapshoot

Worth mentioning, only because so many LOCTs do it. They take a chance and disregard health insurance. Some feel that deductibles are so high, they would be better off saving the premium money, paying any medical bills, and hoping for good health.

Uninsured LOCTs get by every day. The question is how much risk are you going to—can you—take. The risk problem compounds because once you go without insurance for a while, without incident, getting a policy becomes less and less of a priority. Not only would a major accident be costly, but it may also hinder your ability to buy insurance after the fact as you would be in a higher, "risk-taking" category. Play your cards as you wish, but realize it isn't that difficult or bank-breaking to add a bit of a safety cushion.

IMAGE ON A RAMEN NOODLE BUDGET

With so much happening in the beginning stages of the LOCT life, your professional image may get relegated to the wayside. At this time, you may feel you have all you and your wallet can handle.

Here's the good, frugal news: It doesn't take too much cash to get started on developing the image of a professional entrepreneur. Image doesn't have to be the black pit of start-up costs, and frankly it is an area where some creative frugality can go a long way.

Here are some of the things you'll need to start thinking about when you use small-budget tactics:

Stationery and Business Cards

This is the category where image is everything, usually the first impression you make on a potential client or customer. And it is the area where computer technology can have its most creative impact. You don't need to immediately head into a print shop while you choose from their generic-looking stationery and business card selection, order the minimum (which is probably hundreds if not thousands more than you need just yet), and pretend to be satisfied. With a computer, your local photocopying shop and a dose of creativity, you can be on your way to something uniquely representative of you to get you started. Here are four simple steps to quickly get up and running:

- Simple starter logos can be built from a good font package. Pick a type font representative of the image you are trying to create: whimsical, irreverent, conservative, whatever. Find something unique but easily readable.
- Using a basic graphics program (if you don't have one, you probably have a friend with expertise; cash in some favors), create letterhead and business cards with this font. Keep the look clean and simple.
- Take the final printout to the photocopying shop for a minimal number of copies, whatever you need to get started. If the copy shop is lacking in interesting paper stock options, head to a larger office supply store,

select from the wider range of options there, and have the shop use those. Buy matching envelopes that you can use in the printer as well.

■ Remember to include all key information on your business cards and letterhead: Name, phone/fax, postal address, e-mail address, and web site address.

You're off and running with minimal financial pain and time spent. It's things like this, getting stationery and business cards made, that give us a quick LOCT high, making us feel that this whole self-employment scene is real and we're making progress. And yet this is also an area where it is easy to get hung up, to start overanalyzing everything so that nothing gets done. You don't need a designer logo and professional print job now. You just need something workable and attractive. Learn to separate overexpectations from the basics that need to get done.

The Internet

As discussed earlier, we're the most "Techie Confident" generation to date, so you don't need to hear from me about the potential of the Internet and the necessity for you to get on it. Establishing a web presence (minimally an e-mail address and ideally a web site), puts you on the board.

Dress the Part

Huh? You thought dressing guidelines were left behind in the cubicle? Sort of. Work dress codes are changing so rapidly all over, moving to more casual styles, it's difficult to keep up. Just because you're self-employed doesn't mean sweats should be your standard uniform. You don't have to dress out of Brooks Brothers, but experiment with your own casual, professional look, and find something you're comfortable with.

Actions Are Cheap

While you'll encounter costs that are out of your control, there is one key professional image variable that you do have full control over: your professional actions and courtesy. For example: You should always be on time; in fact, aim to always be a little early.

And remember birthdays and write thank-you notes. Send out notes for any reason: birthdays, congratulations, holidays, new babies, sending relevant article clippings, whatever. In our fast-paced, electronic-driven world, it's these "traditional" touches that will make you memorable.

"If you asked me what I came in this world to do, I will tell you: I came to live my life out loud."

—Émile Zola

5

Loving Your
New Office

**"It's Amazing How Much I Can Get Done
When I Don't Have to Wear Shoes."**

Home Sweet Office. The ultimate fantasy of the 1990s. Get up when you want. Have your morning coffee while sitting by your window amusedly watching frantic stone-faced commuters running to their cubicles. Work in your bathrobe. Play hooky on a daily basis. Get a tan.

Yeah, right. The "home office/working at home" concept is an overrated fantasy of the '90s workforce. Sure, there are definite perks to the home office scene. And yes, most who try it would never go back to Cubicle Land, myself included. But the reality is that if you plan to work out of your home there is another side that you should know about and prepare to meet head-on.

HOME OFFICE TOOLS

When you move out on your own, you no longer can show up at work and have all the latest technological office tools sitting on your desk waiting for you. You have to equip your own business. This isn't a fact to overlook or an area where you can skimp.

Think of your home office as the Mission Control of your self-employed life, the launching pad of your ideas, visions, and projects. NASA is packed with the best, most current equipment available for their orbiting astronauts; take the same attitude with your home office. No, you probably won't be able to afford or even need state-of-the-art office tools at the start. But some planning and well-researched decisions will give you your best chance of success with your LOCT endeavors.

With that in mind, realize too that you really can't make a 100 percent perfect decision on what technology to use. The industry is changing and growing so rapidly. Computers, cellular phones, fax machines, modems, and other technology are improving so fast that new models have outdated old ones by the time you figure out what you want. There will never be an ultimate, permanent home office setup because technology will constantly improve. What does this mean for the LOCT? Apply the "educated enough" theory. Learn what you need to know to make informed decisions now, keep yourself updated as you go, and budget for upgrades.

Don't get pressured into feeling the need for every techie toy on the market, especially when you're starting out. It's easy to get caught up in the sexy allure of technology; the image of working on the beach with a cell phone and state-of-the-art fax machines with all the bells and whistles. All the cutting-edge, hip advertisements touting the potential of technology can easily manipulate us. This isn't the time of your life for a technology shopping free-for-all. Self-employment doesn't give you a carte blanche to go into techno-debt. Research and purchase slowly. Sleep on it. Keep looking at things from the "tool" perspective by asking, "Is this something that will help me expand, grow, learn, and (very importantly) generate income?"

Focus on the key elements first; work your way up as needs and funds grow. Consider this the Maslow's hierarchy of home office needs. Start with the basics and go from there:

- **the foundation:** computer keyboard, central processing unit, monitor, printer, modem, answering machine, basic software
- **the basics plus:** fax machine, voicemail, pager
- **higher ground:** cellular phone, separate laptop, video conferencing hardware, electronic organizer

LIVING THE HOME OFFICE LIFE

The good news about working at home: You no longer have to live by that blue-binder "office policy" rule book you received your first day on the corporate job. Scheduled

In 1992, approximately 2 percent of the U.S. population had e-mail access. In 1997, 15 percent use e-mail, with growth predicted to grow to approximately 50 percent of the population by 2001.

(*Entrepreneur*, 5/97)

> **PAOS** (Rhymes with "Taos" as in Taos, New Mexico): An acronym for "Perpetual Analysis of Oneself." In order to work effectively in a self-employed situation and in a home office, you need to be constantly questioning and trying to understand how you work best, and how you can work most effectively.

lunch hours from noon till one, dress codes, cubicle decorating restrictions are no more.

Happiness and bliss, you say? Well . . . sorta. The reality is you always work best under guidelines. However, the difference is now you can set those rules for yourself. This is a good thing, but believe me, setting and self-managing your own guidelines are harder and more personally challenging than simply accepting rules that someone else imposes on you.

To create guidelines that will work for you, you need to know yourself and understand what makes you tick. You have to examine your work habits and your daily routine and ask yourself: "How can I be doing this better/more efficiently/with more enjoyment?" Before you set any rules to work by, dig to the core of your personality, biorhythms, and work habits to gain a deeper understanding of how you work best. Then you can create the guidelines that will help you navigate through the often shallow and rocky channels of self-employment.

Perpetual analysis of oneself (PAOS) takes work; it takes constant effort and energy. It also means accepting responsibility for what you don't accomplish, which is often the hardest part to swallow. Now there is no one to blame but yourself; the buck stops here.

The home office scene isn't easy, nor is it for everyone. It takes motivation, self-discipline, and all-around energy. I'm far from the queen of efficiency and productivity, especially when you put me next to distractions like the television and refrigerator. I have to work hard at staying productive and focused.

So how can you adjust to working out of a home office? The best piece of advice is: Be prepared. Understand what you're getting into before you take the plunge. Start thinking about the following issues now, as you maneuver into self-employment.

Timing: Know Your Body Clock and Biorhythms

Let's face it, practically no one works best from exactly 9:00 A.M. to 5:00 P.M. That is a constraint companies impose upon workers for practical reasons.

However, by taking away these corporate restrictions and guidelines, you now face an important question.

The question is not when do you typically work, but when do you work best? This may be a harder question to answer than you think. Maybe you've never really had the opportunity to work in your best environment. But the world is changing, growing away from Clock Restrictions because of things like the growth of self-employment and home offices with computers, faxes, and so on, because of

Clock Restriction: Having to perform tasks at a prescribed time. Usually imposed by an employer or other external source.

> "If you want your dreams to come true, don't oversleep."
>
> —Anonymous

twenty-four-hour services like food stores, banks, printing and copy services, and of course the availability of the Internet, which allows you to jump on the info highway to gather information or chat with others at any time.

Some thought-starters on how you might work best:

- **Night Owl versus Sunrise Lark:** What time of day are you most productive? Two common times are either late night or first thing in the morning. I'm a morning person myself. Not only am I more productive then, but it's a good anti-procrastination technique. If I accomplish my most important, big stuff early in the morning, I'm less likely to get distracted and sidetracked later on. But you may find that you're more awake and creative at night. Go with whatever works best for you.

- **Sleep Schedules:** How much sleep do you ideally need? Test yourself out for a couple of nights. Try going to bed a little early and see when you naturally wake up. And it's okay to develop some weird sleep patterns. I often fall into those, especially when I'm in the middle of a project. When finishing up the last chapters of this book, I sometimes woke at about 2:00 A.M. and wrote through lunchtime, took a nap, and then worked on some other projects. I have the flexibility to work with these schedule quirks, not against them.

- **Jump-start Your Engine:** How do you get into a "flow" work state? Do you dive headfirst or stick your toe in the water slowly? Are you one to hit the ground running, rolling right into productivity mode? Or do you need some time to get started? Again, there's no right or wrong answer here, but it is important to know what works for you.

> **"Ah-ha":** Those moments when your creativity is at its peak. When you are discovering new insights, visions, and perspectives, you are having an "ah-ha" experience.

- **Sprinter versus Marathon Runner:** Do you work best in short intense spurts? Brief but intense flashes of productivity, followed by a short lull before another spurt? Or are you a cross between the Energizer Bunny and the Little Engine That Could? (You keep going, steady and sure, till the mission is complete.)

Your goal here is to identify and understand when and how you get in an "ah-ha" state of mind. There isn't a right or wrong path; it is a matter of knowing yourself and your habits to identify how to get there.

Procrastination: Get Your Butt Moving

I am about to confess an embarrassing, personal problem, a self-inflicted vice that has too often caused me much frustration and lack of productivity. It's the dreaded "moo shoo–itis," a state of being where your body feels like a million pounds of mush. Getting off the couch, or out of bed for that matter, seems like an Olympian feat. Any activity other than opening the refrigerator door or rolling over to reach for the remote control is out of the question. The day goes by. Nothing gets done. I get depressed.

Moo shoo is different from burnout or pure mental exhaustion. You very likely hit burnout and exhaustion while

> "Adults are always asking little kids what they want to be when they grow up because they are looking for ideas."
> —Paula Poundstone

> **Moo Shoo-itis:** A state of being where anything more than getting off the couch is a major feat. The ability to stare at a wall all day and not get bored. While moo shoo-itis may appear to be simple fatigue, it is really a cross between procrastination, laziness, and fear of commitment to a dream. Often involves indiscriminate napping.

working in the corporate world. The weekend rolled around and all you could do was roll over in bed because your brain and stress tolerance levels had been maxed out.

Moo shoo hits us when we should be working at our peak. It hits us when doors are wide open to us, times when we are faced with opportunities and yet can't seem to break through and take action.

Why We Procrastinate Why do we get trapped in moo shoo? Why do we get tangled in such self-defeating traps?

Fear of Risk-Taking. The fear of the unknown can be quite the confining quagmire. We're scared to move forward, so we hang out in limbo.

The Perfection Trap. It is easy to get trapped in the notion that our ideas need to be perfectly formulated and organized before we take action. This way, we think we are never fully ready to move forward on our goals, so instead of making a possibly wrong move, we do nothing.

Poor Self-management. Roots of this problem may have developed on the corporate scene. In those days, your boss may have given you a certain amount of direction on your work: what approach to take, what progress reports to file, and so on. Now that projects are fully on your plate, the game changes and you are the one responsible for identifying priorities, organizing a plan, and focusing. That can get scary and put you in neutral.

Lapses of Laziness. Huh? You thought this book was about ambitious self-starters, motivated LOCTs? You didn't think outright laziness would be a problem? Think again. It is an easy procrastination mode to fall into: You just don't "feel" like doing something. You may claim to be tired, uninspired, need a break, whatever! The bottom line is: You're just sitting on your butt.

How to Kick Some Butt (Yours!) How can you conquer procrastination and get on with your life outside the corporate path? You can read books on time management,

JOSÉ, AGE 28, CHICAGO

"I had no idea motivating myself and keeping focused when I became self-employed and working from home would be such a challenge. I'd turn on the TV in the morning and before I knew it, an hour had gone by while I was watching some mindless talk show. I was getting really frustrated with myself, but then I tried putting some structure into my days by setting a sort of work schedule for myself. I'd work from 10:00 A.M. to 2:00 P.M. (I'm not a morning person), and then start up again around 4:00 and work through early evening. I realized I needed more of a routine to keep focused, and having a specific start time helped. I also realized I had to 'dress' for work. I don't mean I had to put on a suit or formal clothes, but working in sweats made it too easy to roll onto the couch for a nap. I didn't feel like I was 'working' and I didn't take myself seriously. So I'd at least put on some casual clothes like jeans, or khakis, and I found I was much more productive."

some of which may offer you some very solid suggestions. But beware: "Researching" time management can easily turn into a classic procrastination technique. I know because I do it all the time. Skimming and browsing through the organization and time-management books in the self-help section at the bookstore can seemingly be justified because you are supposedly "helping" yourself be more productive.

Nice try. I use that rationale a lot myself to justify an afternoon at my favorite bookstore hangout. Similar to understanding your body clock and biorhythms, the ultimate answer can't be found inside a how-to book, but rather inside yourself. Think about times when you are extremely productive and ask yourself, "Why are these times different from others?" Brainstorm some unique ways to get yourself in a productive mode. Some thought-starters:

- Get into a routine. Oh, don't whine. This is not a nine-to-five gig in a suit. When you don't have anything on your plate that needs to be done at a certain time, it is easy to get distracted in random projects and, before you know it, your day has slipped by. Try getting up at the same time every day. Eat your meals routinely. Schedule your bigger "think work" during your productive times. Try to work out a daily schedule that takes into account your body clock and biorhythms. Then stick to it.
- Focus on small steps. When you're making a major change like leaving the corporate world, it is easy to get overwhelmed by everything that needs to be done. Chill. Take things one step, one day at a time. All of the time-management books out there can be summarized by one simple principle: Figure out what your priorities are and focus on doing whatever is necessary to do first to get you to where you want to be.

Loneliness: The Gang's—Not—Here

No more spontaneous lunch partners. No more ritualized commiserating about weekend social mishaps over a Monday morning cup of java. Although some of your former corporate coworkers may have driven you insane, they at least qualified as interesting distractions.

Loneliness is something that is easily overlooked as a potential problem of home-based self-employment, where social contacts are diminished. The key here is to creatively brainstorm new ways to "connect" with people.

CINDY, AGE 24, MINNEAPOLIS

"When I started doing freelance architecture work and was working from home, I had no idea how isolated I'd feel. Even though all the office politics and petty gossip at my old office annoyed me at times, I missed simply having people around to just chitchat with. So you know what I did? I got a dog. I had always wanted one, but with my former out-of-control schedule at the firm, I knew I wouldn't be able to properly care for a dog. But now, things worked out just fine because walking the dog got me out of the house. I'd not only get some air and exercise, but I met a lot of people—actually, I met a lot of other self-employed people working from home. I put some extra effort into training my puppy when it was small, and that really paid off, because now the dog understands that she can't jump all over my work or bother me when I'm on the phone."

Feeling alone in your home office? Need an inspirational boost? Check out the growing number of self-employed/entrepreneurial web sites that serve as "virtual water coolers" for meeting similar people:

The Idea Cafe: The Small Business Gathering Place
(http://www.ideacafe.com)
Aiming to be "as friendly and casual as your local java house," the Idea Cafe takes a lighthearted, informal approach to connecting entrepreneurs. A wide variety of chat lines, including an "Online Coffee Break," can perk up your home office scene. Check out your "Biz Horoscope" for a chuckle.

American Individual Magazine and Coffeehouse (AIMC)
(http://www.aimc.com)
A gathering place for the self-employed and others following their own path. Check out "The Entrepreneurs/Career Roundtable" to meet like-minded folks, as well as a strong, updated list of Internet web resources.

E-mail. This is my connection mode of choice. I check my e-mail a couple of times a day, exchanging messages with both friends and business contacts.

Scheduled Spontaneity. Your connections with others haven't disappeared, you just have fewer opportunities to engage in spontaneous lunches, happy hours, and so on. Plan ahead and keep focused. Decide ahead of time when you want to get out of the "office," and call up a friend and make plans for lunch. Call up an old colleague from the office to catch up and to see if there might be some potential contract work you could pick up.

The "Well, Since You're Not Really Working" Syndrome

A couple of years ago, when I first started working on my own, my girlfriend Carrie called late on a weekday afternoon. Yes, I was juggling a couple of different projects and deadlines at the time, but I was also working in sweats at home and taking some cookies out of the oven. I was feeling pretty darned happy, a sentiment which was obvious to Carrie on the other end. Carrie, at the time, was working in a high-stress, confining, frantic job in the hotel industry. As Carrie sensed my happy camper situation, she made a flip comment about how "easy" my life was because I "wasn't working."

At first I grew angry. I had been in this situation before, where someone from corporatedom made impertinent, sarcastic comments about my "easy" lifestyle. At first, these comments really hurt, because they made me feel invalid, as if I were living a fake life. But as I grew more experienced and confident in this path I had chosen to take, I was no longer annoyed by the comments. I personally knew all too well where they were coming from and frankly felt sorry for the people making them—sorry because I knew they were passively trapped in a situation they were not trying to change. I knew change was hard. I had been there, done that, bought the T-shirt. I had heard dozens of subtle put-downs like:

- "Can you baby-sit, meet me for lunch, pick up a package, [or other chore] since you're free during the day?"
- "Can you rearrange your schedule, because you are more flexible than I?"

- My favorite: "Can you stay in my apartment today to let in the telephone repairman? I can't because I have to work."

Get used to it; don't boil over. Calmly but firmly react as I did that day with Carrie. I took a deep breath and said, "I'm very busy with my job; I work very hard to have the lifestyle I have."

The Superparent Trap

We all enter the LOCT lifestyle with varying personal histories, priorities, and responsibilities. For some of us, those responsibilities include having kids and starting a family. To parents, the romantic lure of the self-employed life and working at home can be royally appealing. You can do it all simultaneously: be an entrepreneur and a parent. You can be everything to everyone because you are now in control of your life. Wait a minute: Underneath that glossy lure is the reality of continually conflicting roles and responsibilities. As parents, we can give ourselves the unrealistic expectation that we can do it all, and end up no better than before— frustrated, stressed, and tired.

The key is to avoid the superparent trap that says you should be able to perfectly juggle the role of parent and entrepreneur simultaneously. Assess the lure of the home office situation realistically. Don't feel pressured to handle everything yourself just because you're working from home. Try thinking of your role as "parent" as another layer in your LOCT life and then decide what tools and resources you need to best manage this layer. Do you need extra help around the house? A separate room and phone line for your office? In-home day care? These things are now part of your business plan.

TERRI, AGE 26, PHOENIX

Terri had been on her own as a graphic designer for a year before she found out she was pregnant. "My husband and I were planning to start a family, but we knew that we didn't want the kind of lifestyle we'd have if I continued working for a corporation while we were raising kids. My plan was to get my graphic design company up and running before we had a baby," Terri explains. "Then I figured I could work from home and raise my kids at the same time."

That combo of working at home and raising kids proved to be harder than Terri initially expected. "I was trying to do it all; I had just figured that since I was at home, I should be able to. But I finally realized that for me to do both jobs effectively—running a business and being a mom—I needed some help. Now I have a baby-sitter come in three mornings a week. I still am usually home when the sitter is here, but during those times I'm able to fully focus on my work and make phone calls without a screaming baby in the background."

If you don't want to continue paying for child care or if your goal is to spend more time with your children, you might try to incorporate your role as parent as you brainstorm different self-employment options. Perhaps there is something you could do that would be more kid-friendly. Think about options that would enable you to involve both your children and your role as a parent directly in your business. Things like operating a day-care center, teaching children's classes, or designing educational games for kids can give you the best of both worlds.

WHERE ARE WE?

Now we have some pragmatic tools in our pocket as we enter the world of self-employment. We've talked about the basic functions and how-tos, assessed the practicalities. This is where traditional "start-your-own-business" books stop, but that's not the end for LOCTs. You're not simply starting a business; you're creating a lifestyle—your own life, integrating various elements based on your personal values, goals, and interests. In the next chapter, we'll talk about these lifestyle issues, from deciding where you want to live to dealing with long-term financial planning.

CHAPTER

6

Life Planning and Other Important Stuff

"You Mean I Still Have to Pay Taxes?"

Have you ever begun a search for something in your closet only to decide that the whole closet is a mess, so you proceed to pull everything out and clean and reorganize the whole thing? So it goes with the self-employed LOCT.

All areas of your life—the sections of your "closet"—are interrelated and work in tandem with one another to form the big picture of your life. Big issues like where you want to live, how to plan your finances, and how to become an active, contributing member of our society may not seem as pressing as figuring out how to have enough cash flow to pay next month's rent, but they form the underlying foundation of your overall LOCT, the roots to creating a satisfying lifestyle. Don't forget to keep them in mind when you're making your kiss-off plans.

THE SEVEN-YEAR WINDOW

Think about working through the issues in this chapter from a seven-year planning window. Seven years from now, where do you want to be?

Why seven years? When you enter the LOCT lifestyle, you will be surrounded by so much newness and stimuli your perspectives will change. Give yourself some breathing room by not feeling obligated to plan out everything. Close the gap on long-term planning to a more realistic, doable time frame.

Another reason to focus on a realistic time frame is that we're progressing so fast and changing so much in our society that it's growing impossible to predict where things will be in a couple of years, much less in our lifetime. Technology alone, from computer design to Internet capabilities, is moving forward fast and will continue to have a significant impact on self-employment, directly affecting and expanding your work capabilities.

Looking a ways down the road gives you a sense of self-responsibility, of taking charge of your own financial planning and long-term future. This is a fundamental shift from the standard corporate protection umbrella that our parents' generation worked under, the idea that if we paid our loyalty dues, all our big-picture, long-term needs would be taken care of. We'd be able to afford a house, take care of our children, have cushy golden years of retirement. Our generation realizes that this corporate dependency zone is gone, and frankly we'd rather be the ones in charge of and responsible for our own lives anyway.

That self-sufficient, confident, responsible, and independent attitude is the theme of this chapter. You're running solo now, piloting your own course, not waiting for or wanting someone else to take care of you.

Within the parameters of a seven-year planning window, throughout the rest of this chapter we'll examine some key areas to contemplate, such as financial planning, establishing roots, and being a socially responsible citizen.

FINANCIAL PLANNING STRATEGIES

Don't gloss over this section, thinking that the concept of long-term financial planning is way beyond you right now. I know that you're probably worried about deciding what you want to do with your life and how to pay the rent next month, and that's more than enough for you to handle at this moment. However, as a self-employed individual, you are accountable for your own fiscal future. There is no corporate safety net of profit sharing, pension plans, and miscellaneous perks to insulate and protect you; you're now steering your own fiscal security ship.

There are two general tactics many LOCTs use to approach financial planning: They either invest in their own business or they invest in a traditional IRA. Let's take a look at both of these options.

Invest in the Business

This is the epitome of confident self-sufficiency. You are so passionate, so motivated by your entrepreneurial ventures, that you're willing to take any income that comes your way and put it back in the business. You're viewing your business as a tangible investment. With every reinvestment, you see opportunities to progress and grow, to take your dreams and vision to the next level. You're investing and betting on yourself.

That's powerful stuff, and in a way it exemplifies one of the core philosophies of this book: believing in yourself and your abilities 100 percent, tenacity to wholeheartedly go after what you want, a drive to make things happen.

Another way your business can be viewed as a tangible investment is as something you may eventually sell in its entirety for a profit. In this way, the money you invest in the business will come back to you directly as a return. Of course, you get no guaranteed FDIC-insured rate of return, assuming you can sell it. But with higher risks come greater return opportunities.

Invest in Traditional Options

Another approach to financial planning is to utilize existing, more traditional means of long-term financial investments. These are financial savings plans that are advantageous to self-employed people.

Specifically, there are IRAs (Individual Retirement Accounts). What this type of fund does is allow self-employed people to invest money for retirement and get tax benefits today. The amount you put into these funds comes directly off your gross income, lowering your taxable base. Addition-

A great resource for financial planning for our generation is the book *Get a Financial Life: Personal Finance in Your Twenties and Thirties.* (Fireside, 1996) Author Beth Kobliner has created an easy-to-follow, pragmatic resource for our generation to take control of our finances, clean up past debt, and start planning for the future.

ally, the interest rolls over each year tax-free, increasing your rate of overall savings. They are simple to set up (ask any bank or financial institution for information), and you need to put money into an IRA by April 15 to qualify for the deduction from the preceding year. On the downside, the money won't be accessible until retirement (you can access it, but with a severe penalty), and IRAs are the same as money markets and mutual funds in that they are not FDIC-insured.

Which financial approach is best? That's hard to determine because each one of us is in our own unique situation. Perhaps the most strategic way is to look at this from a balanced, diversified perspective. By investing both in your business and IRAs, you're following the time-tested fundamental rule of money management: You're diversifying and lowering your overall risk, increasing your odds of long-term return and security.

HOME SWEET HOME

Where you live, the place you call home, was easier to determine when you were in the corporate world. You probably had one option: You lived where your job was. You could decide exactly where you wanted to live depending on how much time you wanted to spend commuting, but your options were relatively geographically confined.

In the self-employed LOCT world, that changes. Our entrepreneurial generation has the freedom to define our own roots and to create our business and lifestyle around the environment we work best in. We don't have to live in an urban center or some suburb. We can make our decisions based on what qualities we envision for our lifestyle. The underlying issue is that by kissing off corporate America, we have the opportunity to create a lifestyle based on what we feel is important for our personal lives as well as the future of our business.

Now you must ask yourself more of those deep, provocative questions like, "Where do I want to live?" Maybe you really like living where you currently are. That's cool, but if you have never had the opportunity to think about this before, if your location has always been directed by job-specific factors, take the time now, as you start planning your self-employed life, to think about where you really want to be.

There are many personal reasons why people are drawn to live in a particular place. As LOCTs, we have the benefit of considering a range of options, yet our business venture may require us to consider certain criteria. The key to discovering what's right for you is to think through, perhaps for the first time in your life, what your roots criteria are. These are the qualities and resources you value and prioritize, the things that you need in your daily lifestyle.

Here are some roots criteria thought-starters, some things to think about as you brainstorm and research places to live.

Business Climate

Is where you live or want to live conducive to the type of income-generating ventures you're planning? Consider things like:

- Local regulations and zoning requirements. What hoops will you have to go through to get your business approved, if any? Are there existing regulations that you will need to adhere to? Take a serious look at restrictions on home offices. Each locality has various requirements and necessary permits.
- Ability to hire the right employees if you need to. Are there local people who would fit your criteria (e.g., experience, education, personality, etc.)?
- The market. Is there a market for your services or product? Is the market saturated in that area?

Traditional business-climate criteria as we've described it here is important if your venture involves the local market. For example, you're selling to people in the area, employing locals, utilizing local resources and infrastructure, and so on. This typically includes a lot of traditional business start-ups, like retail and restaurants.

However, for a growing number of ventures, this traditional business-climate criteria is less important because the local market doesn't necessarily have anything to do with the needs of the business. These entrepreneurs can work anywhere, thanks to recent advances in home-based technology, such as PCs, Internet and e-mail, faxes, cellular services, and others. Often service-based businesses (e.g., web site design, consulting, editing/writing, etc.) come under this category and will undoubtedly continue to grow in number as technology advances and the overall acceptance of home-based business grows.

Business Support

A related partner to business climate, business support is what you need to "do your thing," the local resources and infrastructure that enable you to do what you do. Business support is often overlooked and neglected as roots criteria, but it provides the fuel to keep your business going.

Business support includes access to:

- photocopying services
- suppliers
- delivery systems (FedEx, UPS, etc.)
- tool/equipment repair services—if your computer broke down, where would you get it fixed? How long would it take?
- Internet service provider
- libraries, research facilities—is there information you regularly need access to?
- network of contacts/clients—are there people you need to meet with regularly, where readily available face-to-face meetings are a critical part of what you do?
- access to professional services (accountants, lawyers, etc.)

Nature/Aesthetics

Now we're moving from the purely pragmatic business necessities to the more individual, personal criteria important to your living environment. These are things we all pri-

CHUCK, AGE 25, CHICAGO

"I thought I could easily locate my web-site design business anywhere, since everything I was doing was via the Internet. So I focused solely on the aesthetics of where I was living and was looking at places out in the country with some land. I think I just got a bit too caught up in the idea of escaping the city and going out in the country, so I overlooked some of the pragmatic necessities I needed to run my business. For example, I just assumed that the phone company would be basically the same as the one in the city. Fortunately, I started asking some questions and found out how wrong I was. I learned that out in a lot of rural areas, like where I was looking in Wisconsin, there are all different small phone companies that can be pretty behind in telecommunications technology. One place I was looking at had just recently gotten the capability for call waiting and voicemail. Also, I've learned that it can be a long-distance call to reach an Internet service provider, which will add up quickly in my business. I still want to move out of the city, but at least now I know to ask the right questions about things that are important to me and my business."

oritize differently based on our own values and needs. But the fact that a comfortable personal fit isn't critical to your business success doesn't mean it is of less importance in your roots criteria. That's the beauty of being self-employed: having the ability to examine your lifestyle inclusively, being

CAROLYN, AGE 27, DENVER

For a long time, Carolyn was an urban dweller with a skier's soul. "I knew living and working the rat race in the city wasn't for me, but when I graduated from school, the job and the pay looked tempting, so that's what I did. Got a job in marketing. That's what everyone else was doing." But sure enough, after a couple of years in the cubicle, Carolyn started looking beyond the city. "I decided to go to Colorado, always had a draw there. For the first year I basically did odds and ends work at one of the ski resorts. Not exactly using my degree, but for once I was truly happy. I skied a lot and learned more about the area. Eventually I was hired on in the resort's marketing department and now sell ski packages at various trade shows throughout the country. I'm traveling, skiing, living in a beautiful place, couldn't ask for more!"

able to look at and evaluate a variety of roots criteria based on what's important to you.

Are you an outdoors person? Do you choose to spend a lot of your free time in natural places, taking weekends to go camping, mountain biking, sailing, and the like? Whatever your activity, if it's important to you to be able to do it regularly, think about places where this will be possible. Proximity to state and national parks, recreation trails, and preserves enables you to throw out the notion that these are only weekend/vacation activities and to start incorporating recreation into your daily life. Likewise, if you've always been addicted to a certain weather climate—the

Florida Keys, the Rocky Mountains, the Southwest—factor that in with your roots criteria.

Experience Immersion

Experience immersion involves putting yourself in engaging, new situations of learning and discovery. Do you crave newness, change, and challenge, and like to be stimulated by the options around you? Do you enjoy being surrounded by other engaging people who are looking for the same stimuli? If so, these factors should be considered when you're looking for a place to put down roots.

Here are some examples of experience immersion. Are any of these options important to you?

KAREN, AGE 31, TAOS

"I've always had a fascination with the Southwest. Every time I went there on vacation, I just felt like this is where I need to be. The climate, the culture, the scenery just all felt right to me. So when I was planning my transition to self-employment, I knew immediately that my first criterion was to move out to New Mexico. My corporate job was in technical writing, which fortunately is something I can do from anywhere. The company I worked for was swamped and in desperate need of help, so I approached them with the idea that I'd move out West and continue to work for them part-time from home. My company agreed to the plan, which worked out great for me, because I could move to this new place, knowing I'd have a consistent stream of income to cover my expenses while I explored some new options for myself."

- university, local community college, or other adult education centers offering various classes and seminars
- ethnic restaurants
- museums
- art galleries
- theater and other performance arts
- various cultural neighborhoods

Home Buying for the Self-Employed

A logical progression that follows planting roots is buying a house, investing in your connection to the place. But first, it's worth noting that home ownership is not the right step for everyone. Owning property brings with it responsibility, financial commitment, stability, and a willingness to learn the real estate ropes. However, for many of us, owning a home is a calculated, anticipated event for a variety of reasons:

- Tax-saving advantages
- Real estate investment appreciation
- Home office deductions
- Having a place of your own, to create your own personal living space through decorating, household improvements, landscaping/gardening, and so forth.

Now the reality check: Buying property as a self-employed person is akin to many moons of slow-drip water torture. It's going to be a slow, drawn out, painful experience. Sorry to sound so discouraging, but the reality of it is you need to be realistic about what you're getting into. The process of home buying can be grueling enough for the corporate consultant with a cushy constant income. It's more difficult when you're self-employed, so just be prepared and ready for what will be at times a rocky ride.

Why exactly is home buying difficult for the self-employed? The current system is against us. The system for mortgage approval and qualification understandably has a variety of criteria for approving a loan application, but a key factor is "consistency of income." The banks and mortgage lenders want to see an even, consistent stream of income directly deposited into your bank account, that is, a salary check. To lending institutions, being an employee (or better yet, a long-term, loyal worker bee at one company) and being dependent on a company for your income is viewed as "safe"—the sign of someone who is much less likely to screw up loan payments. Self-employed people, however, are viewed as risks with erratic incomes.

Of course, lending institutions have a right to be concerned about the risk factor of mortgage applicants. But the status quo system can be frustrating to LOCTs because, frankly, it's the corporate employee who should be viewed as a risky long-term investment. The typical corporate employee could get pink-slipped at anytime, leaving him or her stranded with zero income. Their only means of solving their problem is to throw themselves into the growing masses of corporate lay-off-ites sending out their cookie-cutter résumés.

On the other hand, the self-employed with multiple layers of income generation wouldn't go belly-up if one source of cash flow dried up. They have other options. In addition, self-employed people are accustomed to being responsible for generating their own income, for getting new clients, growing and expanding existing businesses. We're used to being self-sufficient and responsible for our financial future.

But there's no need to ramble on, giving you a laundry

list of reasons why LOCTs are a safer long-term financial bet. You know what's going on. The problem is that lending institutions don't yet fully appreciate us, so you need to toughen your skin and be prepared for what could be a long, tough journey to home ownership.

Given that lending institutions aren't too sweet on the self-employed, how can you buy a house? Here are three general routes to consider:

1. **Play by the rules:** Give the mortgage lenders everything they are looking for: a consistent income stream over a minimum of two to four years and a sizable down payment, ideally 20 percent of your purchase price. No kidding. This is hardly the easiest option, and it may involve waiting longer than you wanted, but it's doable. You can still start your home-buying research process, looking at properties, figuring out your local market, understanding the financial process, and so on during those years of building consistent income. Then when you finally "qualify," you'll be fully prepared and ready to move on something. A big assumption here is that you'll be able to create consistent income at the level that would qualify you for the house you want, but it can be done.

2. **Get some help.** If your long-term cash flow is viewed as "risky," bring in someone with a traditional "consistent" income source to co-sign with you. Typically this person is a parent or relative, someone you already have a trusting, long relationship with. Co-signing is much more than just someone signing her name and doing you a minor favor. The person who co-signs is assuming legal payment responsibility if you screw up. That's a lot to ask of anyone, but if you do have some-

one who you could comfortably approach, it's worth pursuing. The key is to approach the agreement as a business relationship, not as a family favor. Specify any terms beforehand in writing, as any business deal would be handled.

3. **Play the corporate card.** The ironic part to this mortgage thing is that while historic consistent income is important to the approval process, once the note is signed and as long as you keep up your payments, the lending institutions don't care how you earn your income. It can be much easier to buy a home while you're still at your corporate job and go through the approval process then. From the lending institution's perspective, you're the happy corporate camper. This is a trickier approach because you're making long-term investment decisions while your LOCT life is still forming and so much is changing. Are you buying in a price range with payments you can afford? Is this an area where you want to be long term? If you feel confident about your plans and direction, this route may avoid a lot of approval hassles later on.

If you plan ahead when you're house hunting, you can find a place that will not only be a home for you and your stuff but will be a source of ongoing income too. If that appeals to you, evaluate property based on its income generation potential. Two ideas:

1. **Rent space.** The granddaddy of affordable home ownership, taking in renters, is a strong consistent income stream off your property. This can involve either having a separate rental apartment (i.e., a two-flat apartment building or a two-family home) or hav-

ing a roommate who rents a spare bedroom. Or, instead of living space, maybe you can rent out other parts of your property, like storage or workshop space. (Be sure to check the local ordinances on any zoning issues and regulations before you buy based on this plan.) We've got a couple of barns on our property that we rent out for storage space; we also rent some of our land to a neighboring farmer. Renting can have tax advantages as well. Because your rental units are viewed as a separate business, any improvements or upkeep costs to those units are possibly tax-deductible.

2. **Fixer-upper.** Another means of generating income from your property is to invest in improvements and sell it at a profit. This can be a strong income layer for those who are handy with home improvements and repairs and enjoy making them. If you like to work with your hands, look at properties from a "rehab and resell" perspective. Once you get familiar with a local market and finish your first renovation project, you'll have a growing base of knowledge, expertise, and contacts to draw from.

CONTINUING EDUCATION

The LOCT generation is unique because we're lifelong learners. We want challenges and growth opportunities throughout our lives. As you make long-term plans, continuing your education and skill development is a vital necessity to incorporate into your life.

GLOBAL CITIZENRY

The title of this chapter is "Life Planning and Other Important Stuff." So what's the "other important stuff"? It's the contribution to the world we live in, often overlooked and neglected as we plow along in our day-to-day to-dos. These are those things you always wished you had time for when you were in the corporate world.

> "We may have arrived in different ships, but we're all in the same boat now."
> —Martin Luther King, Jr.

This isn't the token end of the chapter, rah-rah pep talk for social service. Throughout this book, the LOCT, self-employed, entrepreneurial lifestyle has been described as a philosophy, a passionate drive for fully experiencing all interconnected aspects of your life. What is a result of this philosophy? You're truly alive, fully living, feeling connected with the world around you. Once this happens, the stereotypical concept of environmental protection and volunteer work takes on a much deeper, more personal meaning. And being self-employed gives you the time, resources, and personal control to do something about it.

Reduce Your Environmental Impact

No big surprise, but our planet is wasting away from our overconsumption. The good news is that as a self-employed person, you're in control of your own office and workplace. This gives you a tremendous opportunity to make positive environmental choices that limit any harmful impact. Perhaps you have always been environmentally conscious at home; you recycle and try to buy eco-friendly products. But now that you are in control of your work environment and work schedule, you have the opportunity to take it up a couple of notches. Be proactive and conscientious when mak-

TROY AND TINA, AGES 28 AND 27, SAN FRANCISCO

Troy and Tina are a couple with a plan. Troy smiles and says, "I'd jokingly say to people that since college I've been working as hard as I can to not get a job." And it looks like it's working. The northern California couple, who got married last year, are working together to develop a partnership of self-employment so they can have the lifestyle they want.

"I'm the type of person who needs to keep my life full of lots of things," Tina explains enthusiastically. She balances several part-time jobs, from outdoor education projects to working with kids to working their large garden. Troy works nights at a group home for troubled youth, which he balances with landscape work during the day. "I really enjoy working outside," he says. "Landscaping, gardening, that sort of thing. The kids at the home are another of my passions. But people will pay me more to mow a lawn than work at the group home, so the different things sort of balance each other out." Troy is looking to take some time off next year and pursue another long-term interest of his: music. He's aiming to spend a couple of months in Chicago studying blues.

Creating a sense of community and establishing roots was also important to Troy and Tina. They now live in an old farmhouse with large gardens on the edge of a university town. "The banks weren't paying any attention to us (with our incomes and untraditional jobs), so my dad helped us out by co-signing the loan," explains Tina. "My dad hoped we'd buy a safe condo down the street, but we love this house. His definition of security is different from ours, but he trusted us enough to co-sign."

Tina and Troy use rental income to help make their mortgage payments. "We have a separate apartment unit we rent out, and we rent a room to Tina's sister and her husband as well," says Troy. "It was an unexpected gift that we love the people we live with so much. We wouldn't want it any other way."

Their long-term goal is to be self-sufficient, creating the lifestyle they want in balance with doing what they want to do. "A key for us is to learn to live on a lot less, " says Tina. Creativity is also a big part of their lifestyle. "Creativity comes naturally when you eliminate distractions, like the TV. I think that's hard to do when you're working eight hours and have an hour commute each night. You're tired and just want immediate gratification," explains Troy.

ing decisions that have an environmental impact. Some thought-starters:

- Cut down on paper use. Buy recycled stock paper; office supply stores today have a wide selection. Use both sides of a sheet of paper, especially for printing draft copies. Use new paper only for final presentation copies. Use e-mail as much as possible and eliminate paper use entirely.
- Reuse mailing supplies whenever possible. Large mailing envelopes, especially the padded kind, can be reused several times.
- Cut down on energy use. Replace energy-draining standard light bulbs with energy-efficient compact fluorescents. Turn off the coffee maker. After you brew a pot, pour the leftover java in a carafe to keep warm and fresh; there's no need to keep the coffee maker running. Keep your home office as well ventilated as possible. You'll use less energy to heat and cool, and your work environment will be healthier.

Real Goods Trading Corp. is a retailer and mail-order distributor of environmentally sustainable and energy-saving products. Their catalog offers all sorts of energy-efficient products you probably never knew existed, all with easy-to-follow instructions. For a catalog call (800) 762-7325 or visit their web site at http://www.realgoods.com.

Become Active in Your Community

Feeling connected to a community is important in establishing roots somewhere. Become involved with nonprofits and civic organizations in your local area. Now as a self-employed person, you can do much more than just write a donation check. With a more flexible schedule, you can have a greater impact by getting involved. You can be active with school groups by teaching a class, or you can work at a shelter during weekday hours, when they have a real shortage of volunteer staff. Learn more about local affairs by attending school board, township, or planning committee meetings.

Turning to the nonprofit and volunteerism scene, check out *Who Cares* (http://www.whocares.org). *Who Cares* is an award-winning magazine (and now a web site) encouraging volunteerism, social activism, and nonprofit start-up among young people.

CREATING YOUR PLACE ON THE PLANET

In a life of self-employment, you are dealing your own cards. You're creating your own hand in the game of life. From your financial plan to your living situation, we're talking about creating your own place in this world, crafting the lifestyle you want. This is in many ways a revolutionary approach to living—rolling personal interests, business needs, and living situations all into one. In the next chapter we'll move into another key element that can both help and hinder your life pursuit: relationships.

"If you assume that there's no hope, you guarantee that there will be no hope. If you assume that there is an instinct for human freedom, there are opportunities to change things, there's a chance you may contribute to making a better world. That's your choice."

—Noam Chomsky

7

Warning: Roadblocks Ahead

"What Will I Tell the Folks?"

Having lived in Chicago, I can attest that half the city is under construction at any given time. Negotiating roadblocks, detours, and orange construction cones, often using alleys and back roads, is a constant challenge.

Breaking out of the corporate scene can bring you up against similar obstacles, only the roadblocks are often people in our lives trying to steer us elsewhere. Managing the pressure from these people is hard, especially if the heat is coming from close loved ones. It is coming at a time when you are vulnerable and in desperate need of genuine support.

Please don't skim over this chapter lightly, rationalizing that it's psychobabble and that you don't need the approval of others. At some point, in some way, you will be dealing

> **Roadblocks:** Hurdles that a LOCT will encounter on the road to life outside the corporate cubicle. Road-blocks can range from well-intentioned family and friends to self-imposed barriers and limitations. Road-blocks are necessary, important obstacles to overcome because they solidify our determination to make it outside the corporate protection zone.

with criticism, self-doubt, and peer pressure, and you'll have to justify your noncorporate life to someone. It's harder than you think to stand tall. And don't overlook the most important roadblock to your success: you. "Who, me?" you say. Ironically, we ourselves can be the major stumbling block to success.

ROADBLOCK NO. 1: FAMILY, FRIENDS, SPOUSES, AND SIGNIFICANT OTHERS

The underlying themes of this book are independence, self-confidence, and going after what you believe in, but there will always be a part of us that wants to be cajoled. There's a part of us that wants to be accepted and loved, that wants the approval and support from the people who are important to us.

You can't blame us for wanting that. Kissing off corporate America is a major life change; we're putting our egos, finances, future—you name it—on the line. Having some cheerleaders around, important people in our lives emotionally supporting and boosting us, isn't too much to ask for.

But approach your relationships objectively and realistically. Be prepared for the likely possibility that not everyone may be there for you 100 percent. You're going through some significant life alterations, and the people in your life may or may not be in sync with them.

Develop what we'll call "realistic relationship expectations." Some people will be there for you completely as you find your LOCT. Others won't be. Accept that. Don't fall into the trap I (and many others) have of wasting a lot of time and precious energy trying to change those people in our lives who will never fully get what we're doing. The only thing you can change in your relationships is your own attitude and actions. Don't put yourself in a no-win situation by trying to get a four-star seal of approval from everybody. Let's look at some relationships—your parents, friends, and SOs, and discuss how these relationships may be affected by your career move and what tactics you can use to keep your important personal connections and still keep focused on your LOCT.

Parents

First, let's acknowledge that we all come from different families with various perspectives on entrepreneurship and self-

Approvalpleez: Our need as LOCTs to have our non-corporate career paths approved and accepted by others. No matter how self-sufficient and independent we are, things would always be better if we had a chorus of cheerleaders at our side supporting us.

employment. If you grew up in an environment where the entrepreneurial sprit was relished and rewarded, and your kissing off the corporate world is fully supported by Mom and Dad, congratulations. And I'm jealous. For many of us going through this process, the support structure we've turned to all our lives, our parents, isn't fully there when we're turning our backs on corporate security.

Our parents mean well. They love us. They want us to be successful and happy. The problem is that our generation's definitions of "successful and happy" differs from our parents'. We're not playing by the old corporate rule book anymore, but rather we're writing our own rules and definitions. Because of this, it's as though we're speaking a different language than our parents, seeing the world through different lenses. Wanting a flexible schedule so you can travel more, living somewhere near good skiing, valuing freedom over financial security—these are things they have a hard time relating to.

Parents' comments may fall into three categories:

1. Criticism of what you're doing: "You're not doing the right thing."
2. Erosion of your confidence: "You can't do that. You'll fail for sure."
3. No comment—asking no questions, talking about anything except what you're doing with your life: "If I ignore it, maybe it will go away."

Why the Resistance? Why is there often so much parental conflict when we're leaving the corporate world? Why can't our parents just "get it"? Now is the time to put on that objective hat and look at Mom and Dad rationally, perhaps for the first time in your life. Some possible reasons parents have a hard time understanding and accepting our kissing off corporate America follow.

The Protective Parent Role. Since the day we were born, our parents' goal has been to make sure we were kept safe and secure, that our needs were met, that no harm would come our way. So Mom and Dad were happy when you got a cushy corporate job. You were being passed from their safety net to what they perceived to be a protective corporate cocoon, complete with a pension plan and dental benefits. Their worries were over, their child was set for life—until you started making waves with your irrational talk of throwing away all this happiness and bliss they worked so hard for you to earn.

Corporate World Generation Gap. There may be only a couple of decades between when our parents entered the workforce and when we did; however, there are tremendous differences between the corporate world then and now.

First, it was probably just dear Dad who had a true career-track job, not Mom. The impact and growth of women in corporations over the past thirty years has permanently shifted the makeup of the workforce. Second, Dad probably saw his entry into corporatedom as a guaranteed one-way ticket to long-term financial success and security for himself and his family.

But (and I know this is not a major revelation to you) things ain't what they used to be. The corporate security blanket is nonexistent, and the protective "family" nature of the corporations of Dad's era has been replaced by a survival of the fittest jungle mentality. Your parents are probably aware of the lack of corporate security via cover stories in major news weeklies and *60 Minutes* segments. But it still isn't as real to them as it is to us. "Oh, don't worry dear, I'm sure you won't be one of those they lay off," Mom may coo. Ignorance may be bliss, but our generation has a bit more of a reality check going on.

I've had a lot of struggles with the corporate world generation gap, personally. As I was going through my "I gotta get out of my cubicle" crisis, my dad was having his retirement dinners after thirty-five years of working as an engineer for the state highway department. In his eyes, the past three and a half decades behind a desk added up to a now secure retirement, steady cash flow, and an all-around solid upper-middle-class suburban lifestyle with all the perks. I was fine with all of that; my dad got what he wanted according to both his and my mom's priorities and values. The problem was it wasn't

"The 'rents definitely wanted fifties lives for all of us. Go to college, get a standard job, get married, have kids, etc. The older two followed the road map. Now, they, and many our age that followed the same, are unhappy and feeling cheated. The older ones either got laid off at the Big Company, or worse, stayed after the layoffs and are working two people's jobs. Their salaries aren't growing. The people that they were dating at the age when they were 'supposed' to get married didn't turn out to be the best mates for life. Me and my little brother and other Xish cohorts saw that all the institutions that we were supposed to build our lives around were crumbling, so we made our way—started businesses, got into new industries, did wild things with old industries. [We] have relationships when we meet someone for whom we have genuine affection, not on a timetable prescribed by tradition."

—Posted in the "Sandwich Generation" folder on America OnLine for me. There was and still is a wide canyon of difference between how we view a career.

Parental Peer Pressure. Every parent wants to receive the gold star of parenting award, to have their children be lauded and admired by all. "My son is a lawyer." "My daughter just got a promotion and salary raise." Corporate job descriptions are easy to explain, simple to understand and digest.

So it isn't easy for Mom when the neighbors ask how's Johnnie doing. "Oh, he quit his account executive job to backpack through Asia till his money runs out and then come back to do something else, we really don't know what." Most likely Mom will say, "Oh, he's fine," and quickly change the subject. Parental peer pressure isn't an easy thing for Mom and Dad to admit to feeling, but it's there, and the "what will I tell the neighbors" dilemma is always running through their minds.

And how does this make you feel? Not too secure in what you're doing anymore. Bad. An outcast. Your parents are embarrassed by you. Maybe you've always been their pride and joy, the Golden Child who could do no wrong—well, no more.

Feeling a Bit Green. Huh? Parents jealous of their children? Not exactly something parents would admit to or acknowledge, but it is sometimes there. The wish they were young again, in your shoes, with the freedom and opportunity to do things over, this time their way. Perhaps they've been a bit burned in their own corporate careers, and the shining gold watch at the end of the career tunnel just isn't there. They may feel like they had to pay their dues and bite the corporate bullet, so you should too.

Managing Parents Take two aspirin and call me in the morning. I wish the solution were that simple. Still, don't let the parents get you down. Believe me, I've had my share of moments, but three years later, I can say from experience that things get better. Hang in there, keep going, and try some of these tactics for reinforcement:

- Remember to keep your "realistic relationship expectation" hat on. If your parents aren't into what you're doing at the start, the odds are against you that you're going to orchestrate a 100 percent conversion anytime soon. Don't waste your time and energy trying. Learn to accept the fact that this is a situation in your life, maybe for the first time, where your parents won't be there to support you. Right now they simply don't have the shared understanding.

- Learn to agree to disagree. This basic concept shed a whole new light on my relationship with my parents. You see, I had been playing the "good girl" role all my life, always did what was expected of me, always looked both ways twice before crossing the street. For the first time, really, we were at a crossroad because we didn't agree on what I was doing with my life. After too many fights, I finally realized that there was no point to these arguments because we simply disagreed. Each side wasn't trying to empathize with or understand the other but was instead attempting to convert the opposition. And it wasn't accomplishing anything except raising already hot emotions to a higher level. If you find you're getting trapped in this cycle, if you're having too many discussions with your parents that go nowhere, just stop. Stop the bantering and say, "Look, we simply disagree on this. We're not going to change each other's minds; there's no use getting emotional. Let's move on." Change the subject. Walk away if you have to. Go to the bathroom—anything—but don't get dragged back into a no-win debate. Agree to disagree.

- Actions speak louder than words. Don't waste time trying to verbally explain what you're doing, just get out there and do it. Focus on what you can control: your actions, your accomplishments. The less time you waste talking and the more you spend doing, the more your parents will start to see the tangible fruits of your ideas. You'll be happier and more confident, which will directly reflect in your relationships with them and others.

- Identify another relative ally. Okay, so Mom and Dad don't get it. Is there someone else in your family who does? Who understands where you're coming from? Maybe a brother or sister? I've got an uncle who has a more realistic read on the corporate scene than my parents; he can better relate to what I'm doing. Not only can he be a buffer between my parents and me, but he helps me feel connected to my family overall; not everyone thinks I've gone off the deep end.

- Surround yourself with other sources of positive reinforcement. We'll talk more about ways to do this in the next sections of this chapter, but the key is to take proactive action and seek out other people in your life to be your positive, "you can do it, I'm behind you, go for it" cheerleaders.

Friends

"I'll be there for you," claims the theme song of the *Friends* TV sitcom. Hey, that's what friends are for, right? But change

BEVERLY, AGE 25, SEATTLE

Bev is aiming to trade in her corporate job for one closer to her heart, working in outdoor education. She knows what she wants; the challenge lately has been convincing her dad.

"I knew I had to get out of my corporate media job before I got stuck with the golden handcuffs," she says. "I went on a Sierra Club trip last year and met the most inspiring people. I came back with a new sense of hope: Leading these types of trips is what I want to be doing," she confidently states. "The more people I met in the industry, the more I was sure this was the right thing to do."

But she's hitting some roadblocks. Her dad is not on board; he doesn't understand what she's doing. As are many people, Bev's dad is of the security mindset: Create a big nest egg, have a cushy retirement plan. Going from a corporate job to one in the nonprofit outdoor ed field is the complete opposite of this, from his viewpoint.

"It's ironic in a way," says Bev, "because I really have saved a lot of money since college, since I've been at this job. I mean, my dad trained me well when it came to the attitude of saving for the future. But I've had to learn for myself to determine how much is enough, and realizing my happiness was more important."

What are her plans? She's taking things slowly. "I knew I wasn't ready to go back to school full-time to get my Master's in outdoor ed," she admits. The decision was still feeling new and green with her; Dad's pressures weren't making it any easier. "I'm going to start classes part-time in the evenings, and lead courses during the weekends. I just know I have to do this, make this change now. I don't want to regret my next twenty years!"

of any kind can put new twists on old friendships, and you are changing, growing. You're not exactly the same person you were.

Again, think "realistic relationship expectations." Think

about some of your friendships; think about how your friends will react to your new life of self-employment and freedom. Don't expect everyone to understand and relate. Appreciate and utilize those who can.

In general, your friends will fall into one of the three following categories:

1. "I Couldn't Do It, But All the Power to Ya, Buddy" These are the friends who will probably never borrow this book from you. They're quite content in their secure, corporate situation, with seemingly no intent on leaving. Yet they are true friends of yours who know you well, and while you may have differing work and lifestyle values, you can respect each other's perspective and support each other's endeavors. These friends are especially important during the LOCT process because they can be an objective sounding board for advice and feedback as you move along. They can also give you necessary nudges to keep going. And, because these are the buddies who still have regular paychecks, they can take you out for dinner and listen to you vent when you need it most.

2. "I'm in This with Ya" (Maybe) As you start your LOCT process and start filling your friends in on your plans, you may be surprised at the number of people who reply, "Really? I've been thinking about just the same thing." Birds of a feather flock together, so why not? It makes sense that many of your friends would be like you, with similar values and interests. Initially, this can be exhilarating, motivating. You and your buddies kissing off the corporate world together, sharing motivations and ideas along the way.

Partners and teamwork can help move your LOCT process along in several ways. There is safety in numbers;

> "Keep away from people who try to belittle your ambitions. Small people do that, but the really great make you feel that you too can someday be great."
>
> —Mark Twain

leaving the system isn't as scary when you have people around you sharing the experience. You can pool resources and contacts, be each other's sounding board, empathetically vent to one another when frustration takes over.

But be cautious when kissing off with a friend. Maybe you've been in this scenario before: You meet a buddy for dinner. You both start bitching about work, downing the corporate scene. You start creatively brainstorming what that "something else" is you could be doing. The energy and synergy at the table feel electric; you hit an idea that really clicks. You head home that night feeling more positive and happy than you have in a long time.

Then what? Truly equal partnerships at this stage are difficult to maintain. If the motivation, time commitment, resource dedication, and so on are equal on both sides, focus on keeping it that way. It usually isn't. It usually isn't one person's fault for dropping the ball, it's just that things always "come up." People get distracted. Reality sinks in. In a way, partnerships lessen your responsibility to yourself and your own dreams. Now there's someone else to pass the buck to.

Just be careful and cautious that the friends in the same boat move you forward rather than hold you back. I fell into the partnership trap with this book for a while. Looking back, I think I was scared of the idea; I wasn't feeling confi-

dent enough to write it myself. So I mentioned the idea to two friends who strongly related to the concept and eagerly jumped on board. We divided up chapters, research, and to-dos. For a while, we were moving along. But things came up in my friends' lives. One started a new job. One went to grad school. And I was left back at the starting line, with me, myself, and my idea. Writing this book myself was much more of a personal challenge, much harder, but I learned along the way that the only way I can fully guarantee that something gets done is to do it myself.

3. "I wish I were you" (Not) The "I wish I were you" buddy is someone who has a perpetual laundry list of excuses as to why they can't kiss off the corporate world:

- "have to still make some money so I can . . ."
- "can't leave my job now because . . ."
- "don't have your connections/luck/etc. . . ."
- "know everything comes easy to you . . ."

These "friends" may more accurately fit into the "acquaintance" category, people in your circle of friends whom you may bump into at parties. They may be displaying a bit of envy here, jealousy that is coming to the surface in the form of jabs, sarcastic comments, and excuses.

You can't really blame them for feeling this way. What you're doing is tough. These acquaintances may earnestly want to do the same thing as you, but they frankly don't have the guts. They can't make that full, 100 percent commitment. They may have some valid reasons for leaving their corporate situation, but more than anything else, they simply can't prioritize and make necessary adjustments, scaling back when necessary.

I've had my fair share of these types of encounters, especially over the past year, when my LOCT started finally falling into place. I was finishing up the book. I had just married my long-term boyfriend and we were ready to move out to the country. My goal of being able to have the freedom and flexibility to travel for long periods was becoming a reality. Life was getting good. At the same time I started getting some snide comments of, "Well, everything comes so easy to you." "You must have some connections, right?" "Your parents must have helped you guys out financially, right?" No, no, and no. The big, dark secret to my success was three long years of planning, saving, and applying myself.

Again, apply realistic relationship expectations. Don't squander yourself, your most precious resource, trying to justify your choices to people who aren't sincere friends. Look to other true, supportive friendships for encouragement and move on.

Spouses and Significant Others

The most powerful, inspiring relationship in our LOCT lives is that of our life partners, soul mates, husbands, wives, boyfriends, girlfriends, and so on. It is these people who know us best, who love us unconditionally and who want to see us be all we can be. Yet just as these relationships are the most impactful, they also have the greatest potential to get bruised or come apart entirely.

Relationships with spouses or SOs obviously cover a wide range of histories, shared experiences, and personalities. From the kiss-off perspective, they seem to fall into the following two general categories:

1. Dual Journey Both you and your sweetie are in this LOCT thing together. One of you may have inspired the other. Or maybe both of you have been on this quest for your life purpose, and you jointly agree that creating a lifestyle together outside the corporate world is the way for you two to go.

You may be partners literally, working together on the same idea. You may have different interests and goals but are overall searching for the same lifestyle and work pattern. Or you may fall into some combination of the two.

There are pros and cons to the dual journey. On the plus side, it can be stimulating and passionate, a greater opportunity to grow close as a couple. You'll be seeing all sides of each other in ways you've never experienced before.

But there can be problems. Two people who have a romantic relationship don't necessarily work well together. Too often a couple will assume they will work well together and neglect to give it a trial run. By taking dual journeys, you're taking on more risk, more uncertainties. Relationships can be tricky enough to maneuver in calm waters. Going into business together can add daily tidal waves. Make sure you both know how to swim.

2. Along for the Ride "Along for the ride" means exactly that. While one partner is pursuing his or her own LOCT, the other is quite content to stay in his or her corporate situation. As we've discussed throughout this book, kissing off corporate America is not for everyone, and sometimes marriages and relationships fall into a split situation.

How does this work out? That depends. Different life paths and interests can cause people to grow apart. With such distinct career and lifestyle interests, with such different day-to-day activities and to-dos, it isn't surprising that you could wake up one day and realize you have nothing in common anymore with the person next to you.

But on the flip side, having these different work goals and paths can add a strong sealer to the relationship. One person is able to go out and take on more risky entrepreneurial endeavors while the other side is taking care of bringing in the consistent income, health insurance, and other life necessities. And who knows—maybe at some point the roles may reverse. Once one person is a bit more settled in his or her LOCT, the other may decide to take the plunge and try out self-employment too.

LOCTs with Kids

And while we're discussing spouses and relationships, let's take it to the next level: kids. Maybe you have some already. Maybe you see them in the near future. Or maybe they are planned for the distant future. How would your life off the corporate path affect your role as a parent? As with so many other issues we've discussed, there are pros and cons and lots of gray areas. You're making these LOCT changes to be happier, to create the lifestyle blend where you have the elements to be your best. People who are going after their dreams are inspirational. You're the role model for your kids; the fact that you are passionate about what you do and the life you lead makes you the most positive, inspiring role model you can be. But being a LOCT parent comes with its share of challenges. LOCTs live a life of chaos and ups and downs, financially and emotionally. It's one thing to be responsible for yourself, or even a partner or spouse. But once you enter the realm of parenthood, you enter the highest ground of responsibility. You're fully responsible for another person. Have a plan and don't take parenthood lightly.

ROADBLOCK NO. 2:
THE MEDIA AND SOCIETY

"As if I didn't have enough roadblocks already, you mean society is out to get me too?" Don't get paranoid, but do have a realistic view. Perhaps not as pervasive as the direct, day-to-day relationships in your life, the influence of the media and societal expectations runs deep.

Television, school, magazines, movies, advertisements, and other media all give us technicolor imagery of the ideal life and what life should be like once we've "made it." Have you felt these expectations?

- happily married to Mr./Ms. Right
- own your own designer home
- drive a nice car
- picture-perfect kids with more on the way
- travel to exotic places
- designer wardrobe
- aerobicized and nautilized body

What? You mean your life doesn't include this list of wonderment? Surely you must feel incomplete, incompetent, and way behind in your life expectations.

Yeah, right. Of course we know better. We don't develop inferiority complexes with every late-night cable repeat of *Thirtysomething*. But still, societal expectations are constantly there of what we are "supposed" to be.

The media and society give lip service to the concept of creativity, innovation, and entrepreneurship. They love to laud the image of the risk-taking, bold, confident pioneer, yet underneath it all, the status quo is what is continually and consistently rewarded. Maybe you saw this in the cor-

MARY, AGE 27, SEATTLE

"I never thought I was so manipulated by consumerism, but I guess I am. The first year I was self-employed, I was doing a lot of different things: writing articles trying to get my freelance career up and going, working on a book proposal, developing my photography skills so I could add images to my writing work. And I was waitressing nights to pay the bills. Needless to say, I had no money to spare. I was fine with that because I was doing what I wanted to do, until I started wandering into stores and saw a new suit or pair of shoes. I was getting too tempted; it was too easy to charge something I didn't need for no real reason. So I basically avoided malls and mindlessly wandering in stores. It just wasn't worth it, and I needed to keep focused on my big picture and what was important to me."

porate environment you were in. Perhaps the big recruiting song and dance you were given resonated about how they like to hire people who think "entrepreneurially." Management may have lauded how innovative and original the company was, yet what was the reality?

Figure out how to unlearn the system you spent your life learning. Seek out new ways of looking at society and media that will help your LOCT quest, not block it.

Find New Role Models

An effective tactic is to seek out and develop new role models, new mentors. There are people out there doing what you want to do, successfully living the self-employed life. You're going to have to seek out and find these mentors yourself. What would this role model be? He or she may be different things to different people, but ideally it's someone who exudes LOCT characteristics, who has created a personally satisfying lifestyle—that is what you're aiming for.

Where can you find new role models?

- Check out your local newspaper or other publications for profile pieces. Potential role models often make interesting feature material because of their variety of interests and projects on the plate. Sunday papers and lifestyle sections tend to publish these stories.
- Network and ask around. Once you enter into the LOCT scene and go public with your plans, people will start responding with, "Oh, I have a friend who did something like that" or "I know someone you should talk to."
- On a national level, magazines such as *Entrepreneur* and *Success* have many feature articles on self-employed entrepreneurs. Drop them a line. You can contact them through the business address, which is usually mentioned in the article, or through the magazine itself, or through the e-mail address of the author or interviewee, if it's given in the article.

Turning off society's expectations is easier said than done, but we can learn to toughen our skin a little. Ignore glitzy TV images and advertisements. Go cold turkey on

GQ or *Cosmopolitan.* Turn off the images the media is feeding you, and instead focus on yourself and where you want to be.

ROADBLOCK NO. 3: YOU

I created many roadblocks for myself when creating the book you now hold in your hands. The idea started germinating in my mind when I first left the ad agency in early 1993. I had just left a corporate situation and felt bombarded and overwhelmed with a range of new options, and I was daunted by where to start. I only knew there had to be something else out there for me. I kept surfing the pop psych/self-help section at the bookstore looking for something to give me a bit of solace, advice, and motivation.

There was nothing out there in the kiss-off-corporate-America realm. So I started playing around with the book idea, ran it by some friends, and received a good response. I put a couple of thoughts on paper and stuck them in a file. I had started a rough book proposal, the seed of a bigger idea.

Over the next two years I whined and prattled on about this great idea I had, "If I could just finish the proposal." I even tried to recruit a couple of friends to get involved and make this a group project. While my friends were capable and generally motivated by my idea, no progress was made because I overlooked one major element: It was my idea. I was the one who needed to passionately live it, feel it, breathe it, and dream it, if it was ever to get on paper. Creating a team project and involving friends was appealing because it lightened my load. But what I was really doing was passing the buck, dividing the responsibility so I was no longer accountable.

So I realized that this would be a solo venture. I start whining again about not being able to finish the book proposal. My song-and-dance routine was beginning to annoy my friends. Supportive encouragement turned to decrees of, "Well then, just write the damn thing." The final impetus was when my boyfriend, John, told me bluntly, "Fine. Don't write it. Just realize that one day you're going to be poking through the bookstore and you're going to see your book idea written by someone else. And you're going to have to live with that."

Ouch. John pulled out his best motivating tactic and it worked. Competition struck a nerve in me. I finished the proposal, and after several rounds of revisions and lots of education about the publishing industry, I landed an agent and then a publisher. Pop the champagne.

You can conquer roadblocks you create for yourself. Let's start fresh: You say you've got a plan to get yourself out of the corporate scene and into the world of self-employment. You've realistically thought about it and are ready to start moving. What are some roadblocks you might unwittingly create for yourself and how can you plow right through them?

No Deadline and No Time Constraints

Think about it: In most realms of our lives, we are given deadlines we must meet. In college, whether you were meticulous in keeping up or if you were famous for last-minute cramming, you took the exam and finished the coursework by the end of the semester. On the job scene, you have status reports and progress plans due at certain times. When it comes to our own lives, however, there isn't a guiding "force" above us nudging us along to completion.

RAOUL, AGE 24, PORTLAND

"I knew I needed to get out of my banking job and into something more creative, more 'me.' Every day, it seemed, I had another big, burning idea. I'd be way into it, start doing some research or make some calls; however, the minute I hit my first barrier, I'd give up on that idea and move on to something else. Looking back, I think I was just scared of making the change. I wanted to do it, but I kept screwing myself by not seeing any idea fully through. Finally, after some time went by and I was really ready, I approached things more pragmatically. I researched ideas fully, brainstormed creative solutions when I hit walls. I'm still at that stage of working out my plan, but now I'm finally really working at it, versus running all over the place getting nowhere."

The same holds true for busting off the corporate path. Your dream is out there, somewhere, maybe somewhat fuzzy around the edges. You get together with a friend for a round of lattes on Saturday morning and start bitching about work. Before you know it Saturday is over, another free day gone and no progress made. Then you're married with children driving a station wagon or minivan, living in the suburbs, trapped in a corporate situation that's much harder to get out of. No outside force is setting a deadline for the completion of your kiss-off venture. It's up to you.

What can you do to help you set and stick to deadlines? Here are some ideas:

Write It Down Yeah, yeah, this isn't exactly a revelation. But you know what? It works. Open up your calendar, decide on the date you want to resign, and write it down. In red. Bold. A noticeable reminder. Be a bit cautious if your calendar is something your boss can see. Get creative and make up a code name.

If you're already out of the corporate environment, take it a step further. Don't overwhelm yourself by setting up an organized and exact plan for the next ten years, complete with tidy intermediary goals on a bar graph. Just take your plan to the next step. Think about some of the issues raised in previous chapters and pick a specific goal that is challenging but realistic for now. Again, write it down. Write it on a Post-It and stick it on the bathroom mirror. Keep reminding yourself of what it is you're focused on.

Write Your Resignation Letter Compose your resignation letter to your current employer. Predate it if you know what the date will be. For some added mental therapy, try writing two letters: one for the record, the one that will go in your personnel file, the one that ends your career there on a good note. Then write a second letter, the one where you spill your guts and from the heart tell your soon-to-be-former employer how you really feel. No holds barred, just the "kiss off" truth. It's cheap therapy and it feels good. (But do be careful not to mix up the two letters!)

Tell Your Friends First, tell your best friend. Tell the one person guaranteed to be most supportive. Whether it's your significant other, spouse, old college roommate, or best friend since grade school, tell that person your big-picture plan and date when you will put it in motion. Give them the exact date you are going to resign. Tell them to write it down and remind you of the fact. Make plans to go out to dinner together that night and celebrate.

Invest or Spend Some Cash For some people, it isn't until there is cash on the line that something becomes "real." Investing the green stuff will get you moving.

What are ways you can "invest" in yourself? Here are some ideas. And remember to organize and save those receipts. Some may be deductions in the world of self-employment, things like:

- a "how to write a business plan" class at a local community college
- an exploratory trip to a place where you're thinking of moving—this is not a vacation, but rather a business trip
- a GRE/GMAT/LSAT review class, for those of you who see a grad school interlude in your future
- equipment you may need in your self-employed world. Think about a relatively significant, useful purchase, perhaps a computer or fax machine. Don't incur a large debt; the goal is to start feeling that this decision is real.

This idea doesn't work for everyone; it only works for people who have a hard time parting with their money—like me. Last summer, I grew enamored with the idea of completing a triathlon. I talked about it but didn't do anything until I invested in joining a gym. I wasn't making a ton of money at the time, so it was a fair expense for me. But it wasn't until I put money down that I took myself seriously. And I did finish that triathlon.

Have a Friend Hold Something Hostage This is a strange, almost desperate tactic, but it can work. Is there a tangible thing that you love dearly? A prized baseball cap, musical instrument, season game tickets? Find a friend who is true enough and understanding enough to hold on to your treasure until you meet your goal.

> "You can't base your life on other people's expectations."
> —Stevie Wonder

Distraction Dysfunction Disease

Remember the last time you hung out with a two-year-old for a couple of hours? They can be crying one moment and singing the next.

The same thing can happen to us when we're trying to change our lives: We easily develop Distraction Dysfunction Disease. Anything under the sun is more interesting than what we are currently doing. We jump from one random activity to another, keeping our goal out of focus.

DDD can sneak up on you in two key forms:

> **Distraction Dysfunction Disease (DDD):** Becoming easily distracted by and engaged in extraneous activities that have nothing to do with your end goal. It is filling time with mindless, unfocused, unnecessary distractions that make you feel "busy" but don't move you any closer to your end goal. Cleaning the closets, saying yes to any spontaneous invitation that comes along, mindlessly surfing the Internet are all classic examples of DDD.

"I wanna play" Face it, there are a lot of temptations around to distract you. And if you had an active social life before, it's going to be harder to say no and focus on your big-picture goal. There are always friends meeting for a beer, watching the game, calling with the shopping or vacation deal of the century. Want to catch a Saturday afternoon matinee?

It's hard to say no, especially when we're feeling frustrated with our lives and unhappy with our job situation. We get in self-sympathy mode. It is the "I deserve this" mentality: I'm having a life crisis so I deserve an evening out, entertainment, whatever.

But these "fun" temptations do dual damage to your ability to achieve your goals. Number one: They are a financial drain. Number two: They steal chunks of time. Friendships and relationships are important in anyone's life, but your priority now needs to be yourself and your future. This tactic may sound selfish, but that's okay for right now. Missing some social functions won't be the end of your friendships. But procrastinating on your future is something you'll undoubtedly regret.

"I wanna work." Huh? We're talking about getting out of an unhappy job situation. Why would you rather work in the corporate world? We can easily set ourselves up for failure by becoming wrapped up in our corporate jobs because we "have no choice," and the days turn into months turn into years. What you're doing is hiding deep within your corporate cubicle, coming up with all sorts of excuses as to why you can't come out, yet at the same time whining about your situation. This helpless "woe is me, I have no control over my life" attitude will keep you stuck where you are. And then a corporate carrot stick may be dangled in front of you, thus creating a trap that snags you and holds you in your corporate situation.

But don't be too hard on yourself here; work can be an easy trap to fall into. In the corporate world, and in our society, work is often viewed as your identity, what makes you who you are. Take away that account executive title, take away a place to be every morning at 9:00 A.M., and in some ways you have stripped yourself of your sense of self, your purpose. That can be scary because you now have to deal with your raw self, with no cushy corporate padding. You are exposing your vulnerability and your ego; you're basically putting yourself on the line by leaving. Be ready to push past this.

Reasons for DDD Why do we set ourselves up for failure like this? Why do we escape into play or work, or a combination of the two? It could be:

- **Fear:** We're scared. That's it, say it: scared. It's ironic in a way. Here you are, the up-and-coming corporate executive, able to swim with the corporate sharks and survive unscarred, you can negotiate and strategize like

Corporate Carrot Stick: A stereotypical corporate reward (i.e., raise, promotion, new job offer, miscellaneous perk) that seems to come right at that time when your personal confidence in kissing off corporate America is shaky and will cause you to reevaluate your plan. Beware: These carrots will often come up when you use work as an escape from your self-employment plan. You're engrossed in work, you get a perk, and your dreams start falling by the wayside. That is, until you have your midlife crisis and flashes of the dreams you left behind haunt you. Don't let that happen; keep focused on your dreams.

nobody's business. You can talk the entrepreneurial talk, but when it comes to taking the first steps of action on your own, you're scared.

- **Lack of Commitment:** Kissing off corporate America is not something you simply dabble in. It's not a hobby you can pick up on alternating weekends, or something you can buy in a preassembled kit. It is a lifestyle change, a commitment. It is being able to say no to situations that might sway you. Not easy to do.

- **Insecurity:** You may see all kinds of quizzes and self-evaluations on whether or not you would make a good entrepreneur and if you are destined for the world of self-employment. But there really is only one vital criteria: a gutsy, no-holds-barred 100 percent belief that you can do it. It isn't just intelligence, connections, or money. It's a sassy confidence in yourself and your decision, and having the faith that you can deal with consequences along the way.

Eliminating DDD What are ways to eliminate and overcome DDD in your life? How can you stay focused and productive? Eliminate distractions. This is a pretty basic concept but something that must be done in order to focus. Some elimination thought-starters:

- **Unplug the television.** Store it at a friend's house. It is amazing how much productive time the television can steal away, even if you claim "but I don't watch that much."

- **Watch out for weekend couch-potato mode.** Even if you've left the corporate workforce, you still probably look at the weekend as your fun time. Nonwork time. Sleep-in time. Well, it's time to kick the habit. In the world of self-employment, weekdays and the weekend blend. Your work, life, and all elements in between are interrelated, so a lot of your old rationales (excuses?) don't work anymore. Break the habit of sleeping in and letting the day slip by quickly.

- **Be cautious of mindless Internet surfing.** While the Internet is unquestionably a powerful tool, it can also be a distraction. Try to objectively evaluate your Internet use; put some time limits on random surfing. We're living in an era of information overload. We are being bombarded with more infobytes than we could ever process or need. The key is to start learning how to be selective in your informational intake, to utilize the Internet as a proactive tool and not as an entertainment medium.

- **Maximize your productive time.** Gain an understanding of when you work best. Early morning, late night, with music playing or incense burning—whatever works for you is fine. The key is to understand what your key productivity elements are and to work with them, not fight against them.

Boost Your Confidence with Baby Steps Confidence doesn't come in one brilliant flash of lightning. It grows slowly, building with every action you take. Think about that feeling you get when you're on a roll. Things are clicking along, you're feeling productive, you've got many irons in the fire and they are all fitting together synergistically. That's the feeling, the energy you want to have going as much as possible. And it all starts with one step—a baby step, if need be, but just do something. One action. Do something. Place one call. Write one letter. Do something related to your end goal.

> **Self-employment Dominos:** It's a chain reaction: The more action you take toward building a life outside the corporate cubicle, the more success you will have, the more your self-confidence blooms, the more you will get done.

Then keep this energy going hour to hour, day to day. One way to do this is to remind yourself of your accomplishments on a daily basis. Start a notebook and every night write down a list of everything you accomplished that day. Write down everything, from placing that important call to a future client to taking the car in for an oil change. Focus on what you have done, keep the dominos falling day to day.

Overplanning, Overthinking, Overovering

We can all be perfectionists and compulsive at times, wanting everything to be just right and to have all of the ducks in a row before we take action on anything. Attention to detail is fine, but it is also easily used as a self-imposed roadblock. Some key examples of "overing" are:

- **"I need to do more research."** You always have one more fact to find, another source to check, another person's brain to pick. Whatever you are working on is never finished, it is under perpetual construction.
- **"I have too many ideas."** Every day you have a new idea for your LOCT life. You're busily leapfrogging from brainstorm to brainstorm. And you end up with lots of half-baked efforts and nothing concrete.

- **"After I (fill in the blank), then I will (fill in the blank)."** The timing isn't right. You need to save more money. You need one more promotion at work. You need to wait until your apartment lease expires.

What you need is a better excuse. The timing will never be perfectly right. There will always be something. Even if it appears that your coast is clear and free, something will come up unexpectedly.

You probably can come up with even more "overing" excuses. It's easy to get stuck in this mode because "overing" can always be justified and rationalized.

Some suggestions to nudge out of "overing":

- **Ask some objective friends if you're overanalyzing.** Most likely, they will provide a fresh perspective and tell you bluntly to stop thinking and start moving.
- **Get comfortable talking about your ideas.** Learn to go public with your idea when it is still a little green, a bit rough around the edges. By getting yourself and your idea out there, you will learn from the feedback, thoughts, and resources of others.

8

The Colorful Palette of Self-Employment

"Do I Get A Life Preserver Before I Jump?"

Here we are, the kiss-off final chapter. Pop the champagne. Hallelujah. This is the chapter that will put everything into perspective, give grandiose profound advice, and send you off starry-eyed into the world of self-employment, life-fulfillment, positive cash flow, and eternal happiness and bliss. Yeah, right.

Reality check: There is no ultimate end to the self-employment process. There is no singular magical moment when the curtain goes up and your perfectly choreographed and orchestrated postcorporate life appears. Like the Energizer Bunny, your pursuit of life off the corporate path keeps going and going. There isn't a last chapter, but rather an acceptance that change is constant.

Kissing off corporate America is a lifestyle commitment, a change in attitude and philosophy that will be the backbone of your life from here on in. It's a challenging creed to live by. Prepare to be plagued with self-doubt, sprinkled with that feeling of "Who am I to ever think I could pull this off?" And then to experience a small victory that will give you the courage to stretch further. Prepare to accept that there is no definitive right or wrong path. The key is to have the courage, the passion, and the confidence to keep moving.

AFTER THE CORD IS CUT

This confidence is especially tough to muster in the weeks and months immediately after your kiss-off. This is a challenging period of transition. It's that phase between the security of a corporate paycheck and the ability to pay your rent in the self-employed world. It's waking up in the morning with this agonizing feeling of "Oh my God, what have I done?" which is often followed with a flash of paranoid "Who am I kidding to think I could pull this off?"

This can be a long, bleak, and agonizing phase of bust-

Transitioning: The time period when you're no longer corporate and not yet fully self-employed. You have left your corporate job and are in the initial stages of acting on your self-employment plan. Transitioning is that phase where your world is turned upside down, and you're feeling both frightened and exhilarated at the same time.

ing off the corporate path. The "bleak midwinter" of kissing off corporate America when everything feels cold, gray, and depressing. Prepare yourself. Everyone goes through it. It's a commitment test in a way, because this is an easy time to just say screw it, this isn't working out perfectly, and get sucked back into the corporate world.

Transitioning can last a while. For a lot of LOCTs it is at least a year. It's a phase where you'll go through a battery of commitment tests, quizzing yourself on just how badly you want a self-employed lifestyle. Do any of these commitment tests sound familiar?

- You randomly hear about a job opening, often the same type of job you left. You could easily get the job and fall back into your old safe and comfortable lifestyle.
- The gang is taking their annual ski trip to Colorado. And you know you can't go. The money isn't there. You start developing an incurable urge for pricey Brie cheese.
- Your mother calls for the umpteenth time asking, "What are you doing with your life?"

You're feeling the urge to crawl in bed and hide. What can you do? Take a breath. Reread the "Dreamfunder" section from chapter 3 and rehash and brainstorm some quick money-making options. Review chapter 7 on handling the roadblocks. Keep going. Remind yourself that you have to go through this. You're getting there. Everyone goes through this to some degree. You're growing, learning, and challenged in ways you've never experienced before. Relish these Ramen Noodle days; they are the keys to open the doors of whatever is next in your path.

Still, you can equip yourself for transition limbo. The most important tools you can take with you into this stage are a variety of pragmatic, realistic options. The more options you have out there, the more pots on the burner, the more you ensure your chance at success. Review the stepping-stone ideas from chapter 3, and remember to work in multiple layers so you keep a variety of options open for your self-employment job description.

OFF THE STRAIGHT AND NARROW

To mentally survive and thrive in a life outside the corporate cubicle, throw out all your preconceived notions of career paths. Dump the concept that your life and career will continue along in an easy, prepackaged, "This is what you should be doing now," linear progression. It won't. It can't.

Instead of a career progression from point A to point B, think of kissing off the corporate path as a series of busting phases. Instead of tormenting yourself with the question, "Am I there yet? Have I made it?" ask yourself, "What phase is this?"

The idea of a life without imposed structure and expectations takes on a romanticism akin to running out of the classroom on the last day of school. You're free, in control, time on your hands to do as you please. True. But beware: An overdose of freedom can lead to stagnation.

Stop and think about this. If you really must follow a linear path, think hard before you leave your corporate sit-

Busting Phases: Continual cycles of self-development and education that occur in a life of self-employment.

> **Roller Coasting:** Living with highs and lows, ups and downs, spiced with serendipity. It's the day-to-day life of a self-employed, entrepreneurial corporate buster.

uation. Kissing off may not be for you. For most busters, the peaks and valleys, ups and downs, managed chaos of their daily life are the tangible signs of successfully kissing off. Life becomes a roller-coaster ride and bungee jump all combined. It's kind of tumultuous and kind of crazy, but it's a life of passion and fulfillment. This roller coasting is more than a phase, it is an end goal. It's a lifestyle and a philosophy. This up-and-down, high-and-low imagery should get you excited and pumped, ready to get out there in the world of self-employment.

THE SELF-EMPLOYMENT PALETTE

By now you get the big picture: Kissing off corporate America does not involve a neat, simple, organized list of to-dos. There is no specific pattern of beginnings and endings. It isn't something you think about only from nine to five.

This is a lifestyle, a philosophy that umbrellas your day from the first cup of coffee until Letterman. A drive, a passion, that enables you to ignore societal expectations and say "I want to live my life by my rules, my way."

Self-employment and kissing off corporate America is inherently an art. There is no set of rules, no tested formulas. If there were, there would be a lot more people turning in their resignation letters. It takes courage to be an artist,

> **Life Palette:** The various elements, the tools, of your life that are equally important and interconnected.

to create your own self-employed life, and to be able to share it with the world confidently and say, "This is me. This is who I am."

Self-employment and the LOCT lifestyle are self-expression at its core. You are creating with your own vision, ideas, creativity, and resources your life journey, the path you want to take. Like any piece of art, it is created over time, as your experiences and understanding evolve.

Consider yourself an artist, crafting your life in the self-employed world. Think of the tools you need to create this, the sources from which you draw your inspiration. This is your palette, your Life Palette. Like the traditional visual artist, the elements of your Life Palette blend and merge together in different combinations to create the big picture, the final product.

As you splash color into your work through self-employment, think about the other colors you'll want to also include on your palette. As you read the following sections, think how you'll integrate your mental and physical wellness, your relationships, and your life of inner reflections into the LOCT days ahead.

Wellness

Eat right. Get enough sleep. Drink water. Avoid sugar and fat.

You've heard all the general guidelines for a healthy lifestyle time and time again. But these issues are vitally important in the LOCT lifestyle because:

- You don't get paid for sick days.
- You can't easily call in a substitute.
- Your energy level is a key factor in a successful, self-employed lifestyle.
- You can't simply escape for a couple of days and disappear.

Forget about taking "mental health days," those days you called in "sick" when you weren't. But think about it, why did you need a "mental health day"? You were escaping, literally running away from your corporate situation for twenty-four hours because you couldn't handle being there. Your brain was drained; you felt empty inside. Or maybe you needed to catch up with the rest of your life. Your corporate job duties had taken over most of your waking hours and you needed a day of escape just to catch up on dirty laundry, unpaid bills, dried-up houseplants, and neglected cats.

No, self-employed people can't just call the boss and say I'm not coming in today. But here's the good news: You won't want to. Think about it: If your overall Life Palette is in sync, you are passionate about your day-to-day projects and endeavors. Why would you need to escape and run away? It's not exactly brain surgery, but people blinded by corporate situations can't see it. It's a key difference. You are waking up with a passion for what you're doing.

In the LOCT lifestyle, you will have created two important opportunities: better flexibility and control of your schedule, combined with a strong personal desire to keep your health and energy level high. By having a flexible schedule, you'll have more opportunities to stay healthy and maintain a sound lifestyle. Your workout routine no longer needs to be regulated by corporate hours—either a fast workout in the early morning or after work, when you're mentally and physically exhausted and you're more attracted to crashing over a *Seinfeld* rerun and Chinese takeout. You now have the opportunity to arrange your schedule, interests, and needs to better suit you. Start working out at the gym during off-peak hours, when you can actually get on the equipment and the whole place doesn't reek of sweat. Some health clubs even offer discounted memberships to people like you who can take advantage of off-peak workout times.

Or maybe there are other forms of fitness you can now take advantage of. Perhaps you're the outdoors type, and now you can arrange to take off on your bike in the late afternoon. Is there something new, a sport or exercise activity you've been curious to learn? Tennis, yoga, or tai chi? Check out your YMCA or your local park district or community college for some low-cost class options. Maybe you've wanted to participate in a group activity, such as softball or volleyball, but you knew you'd always end up missing half the games because of work conflicts? Now's your chance to take advantage of things you missed out on while working the corporate scene.

The same flexibility and control of your schedule can enhance your eating habits. You are no longer a slave to erratic corporate meal schedules. We're all guilty of trading a serene, relaxed, and balanced meal for a Starbucks double mocha to go or stale leftovers from yesterday's take-out deli concoction. But now a renewed interest and commitment to your health is vital. As a self-employed LOCT, you have much greater interest in taking care of your number one asset: you. Flexibility and control of your schedule not only give you more opportunities to exercise but to eat better. Working at home gives you access to your own fridge, which eliminates both the need and the cost of constant take-out food. You can better adjust your eating habits to your own biorhythms.

> "If life is a journey, then art is an exploration. To thrive, you must move forward, evolve, and grow."
>
> —Donna Karan

It is this flexibility of schedule and renewed control of your schedule that give you the opportunity for increased overall fitness. But *opportunity* is the operative word here. As discussed throughout the book, control and flexibility of schedules can be a double-edged sword, because now you and you alone are responsible. You can't use the "I was tied up at the office because my boss wanted blah blah blah" excuse for skipping your workout or eating poorly. If you run your system down and are out of commission for a couple of days, you're the one who has to pick up the slack. Motivating yourself can be a perpetual challenge, and it's not something you can hit 100 percent every day. Perfection isn't the end goal here, but rather a daily dedication to taking care of your "boss," that is, you.

Relationships

Another important element in your Life Palette are your connections, your relationships with the fundamental people in your life, the key important people: your friends, family, those relationships that really matter. Not just contacts in the Rolodex, not the people you feel "obligated" to keep in touch with, but the people who have proven themselves to you over time. These are the people who light a spark of inspiration inside you when you're around them, who give you a sense of community and belonging in our fast-paced chaotic world.

These true connections are an area of the Life Palette that can be nearly squeezed out of existence when you're in a corporate environment. Schedule conflicts and self-absorbed business attitudes can slowly strip away true connections.

As a replacement, you might try to find some relationship substitutes at work. Might as well, since you're spending most of your time there anyway, right? Although you can make lasting friendships in a corporate environment, the problem occurs when you find yourself venting all of your problems to the person in the cubicle next to you simply because he or she is there. You haven't had time to connect with your true friends and relationships. These relationship substitutes can be identified by their transitory nature. Sure, they may be nice people and all, but once they or you are transferred to another cubicle in another department, you rarely see them.

Are there relationships you value that you might have been neglecting? Think about your family. Are there some family-related projects you've talked about but haven't been able to act on, such as recording family history, going on a family trip, spending time with elderly grandparents, or finally learning to make that pasta sauce that has been perfected over the generations?

Similar to the fitness aspect of your Life Palette, the flexibility and control of your time can be used to your advantage to keep you connected, grounded. For example, catching a late-night bite after work or coffee on Saturday won't be your only opportunity for connecting. Remember, you're in control of your schedule; you can organize and arrange your life based on your priorities, those key elements of your Life Palette.

By being self-employed, traditional relationship boundaries between professional and personal get a bit fuzzy, in a good way. You may find yourself connecting with all the various people in your life in deeper, more real ways than before. People in your work life are not defined by the restrictive titles of boss, subordinate, or client. Entrepreneurs view these relationships differently. You let your guard down by becoming self-employed, no corporate masks, just the real you. With that, you're able to connect with people intimately, completely.

As you reach out to the world for business, you're building a sense of community that says you are a part of a network, part of a bigger picture. Ironically, corporations try to create an artificial sense of community through imposed corporate culture, from company picnics to contributing to local charities. All well and good, and it is easy to feel a member of that company's "family" for a time. But just as the family unit in American society is breaking down, the corporate family is an illusion because of layoffs, mergers, and downsizing. So take responsibility for yourself and your life: Create your own community, nourish your own connections.

Self-reflection

The self-reflection element of your Life Palette may be the most important because it focuses on the key component in all of this: you. Self-reflection is the continual process of making sure you're on track, going where you want to go. It's taking your soul's pulse, learning how to really listen to yourself and feel at peace and in balance with where your life is.

This is borderline New Age talk, but the ability to take a more holistic approach to your overall lifestyle is one of the fundamental advantages of being self-employed. Self-reflection is an important Life Palette element because it keeps everything else in check. The difference now, versus in the corporate world, is that self-reflection is something you're responsible for initiating and continuing with yourself. You no longer have a boss that gives you annual performance reviews. You no longer have a standard group of peers that you can evaluate yourself against. No more asking, "Am I on track with everyone else?" because you are creating your own unique, personal course. But still, it's important to occasionally monitor how you're doing. Are you on track with your own goals? Are you happy? What steps will you take next?

Everybody has different methods of reflecting; you'll have to experiment to find ways that work best in your new schedule. You might keep some type of written log of your reflections. This doesn't have to be anything too complicated; a simple notebook will do. You're the only one who will ever see this, so don't worry about grammar and the like. You might reflect best by breaking out of your environment and going somewhere different, somewhere you can be a bit objective. This doesn't have to be anywhere exotic, far away, or complicated. A library or coffeehouse will work well. Sometimes self-reflection works well at significant times of the year. These can be holidays, like New Year's, or personal days, like your birthday. High and low moments also offer other opportune times to self-reflect. The two opposite ends of the emotional spectrum let you gain perspective from all aspects of your emotional self.

The point is to stay in touch with yourself. Self-employment can be a hard taskmaster, and if you're not careful, you'll soon be working from dawn to dusk and have no idea what drove you there.

> "And now, for the most dangerous part of the journey
> . . . the return to civilization."
>
> —From the Disneyworld Jungle Cruise ride

Too Much of the Color Blue

Watch out. It's easy to have a bit too much of the "blues" in your Life Palette, the "blues" of feeling burned out, tired, and overall draggy and down. We all have shades of blue from time to time; the palette wouldn't be complete without some blue.

When do the burnout blues strike? Usually when your Life Palette is out of whack and off balance, typically, when you're overworked, running fast in multiple directions; when you're focused on the end goal, when getting to X is the overriding priority.

You probably felt degrees of burnout when you were in the corporate world. Maybe it was when the burnout grew chronic that you were motivated to leave the corporate scene. Or maybe there was one culminating peak burnout experience that was the final straw.

On the flip side, the burnout blues can also hit when parts of your LOCT life may be on a roll, but are out of sync, out of balance with other Life Palette elements. For example, a couple of your self-employment projects may rapidly blast off and become successful and that is where all of your energy, time, and passion are focused. However, other parts of your palette, such as fitness and taking care of your body, may go to pot, and burnout takes over.

> This life is a test. It is only a test. If this had been a real life, you would have been given further instructions.
>
> —Anonymous

However they creep into your life, the burnout blues can be used as a stimulus for self-reflection. They are a signpost, the impetus to take a step back and reevaluate, to connect with your goals and values.

THE SERENDIPITOUS JOURNEY

So after all this planning, after much brainstorming, reflection, research, and so forth, your self-employment LOCT journey begins. You can't see past the oncoming bends, you can't know exactly what to pack, or what you'll encounter along the way, but you're off. You're immerged in a creation that is an evolving, changing, growing piece of art. Like the traditional artist, sometimes things don't work out exactly as you would have liked and you must clear your canvas and start over, take out the eraser and redraw sections. No problem. No piece of art is ever truly finished. It's the process we're aiming for, passionately experiencing the magic of creating a unique and personal lifestyle—a lifestyle that allows for serendipitous moments of unexpected joy you would never experience if you were still on the straight and narrow.

Good luck, have fun, and enjoy the ride!

Have you kissed off corporate America? Thinking about it? I'd love to hear your story—maybe for use in a future book. Please send e-mail to me at LKivirist@aol.com. Thanks!